T. B. Warder

Battle of Young's branch

Or, Manassas plain, fought July 21, 1861. With maps of the battle field made by actual survey, and the various positions of the regiments and artillery companies placed thereon

T. B. Warder

Battle of Young's branch

Or, Manassas plain, fought July 21, 1861. With maps of the battle field made by actual survey, and the various positions of the regiments and artillery companies placed thereon

ISBN/EAN: 9783337730383

Printed in Europe, USA, Canada, Australia, Japan

Cover: Foto ©ninafisch / pixelio.de

More available books at **www.hansebooks.com**

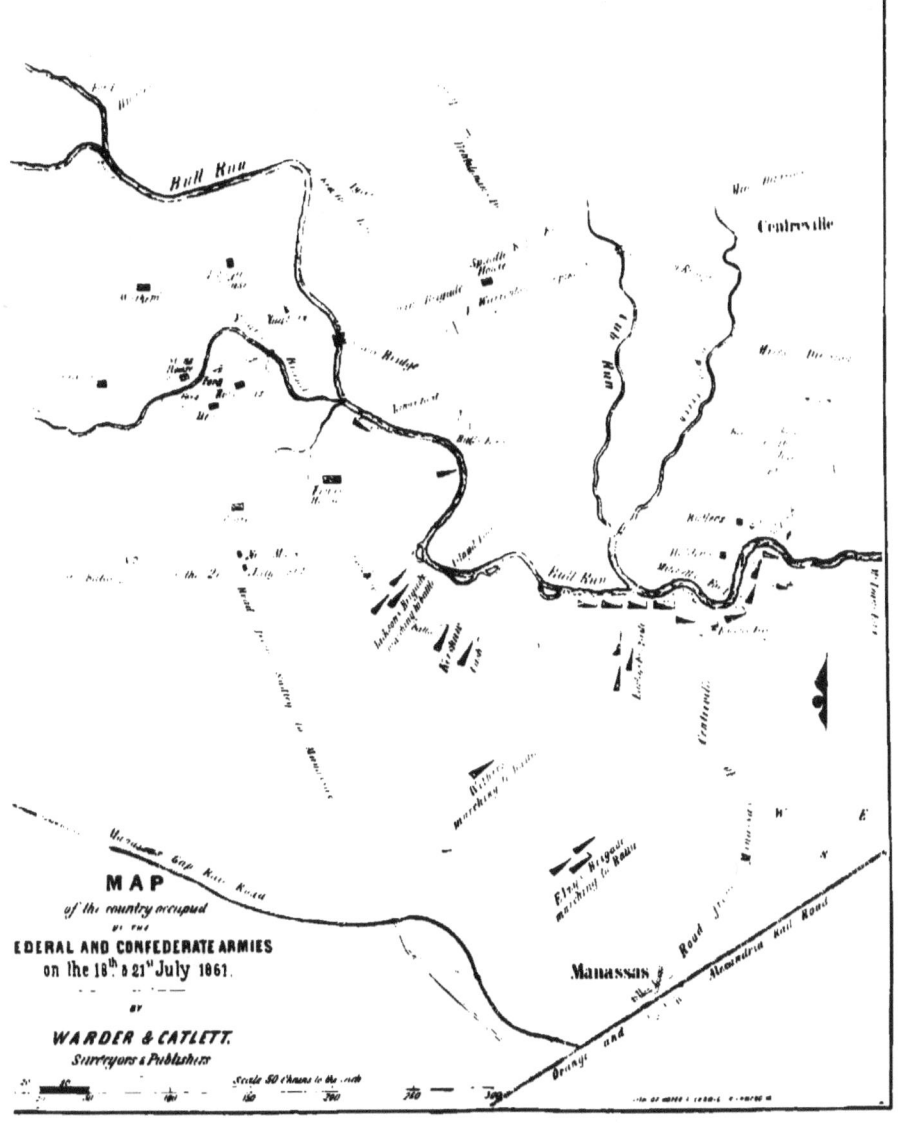

BATTLE OF YOUNG'S BRANCH

OR,

MANASSAS PLAIN,

FOUGHT JULY 21, 1861.

WITH MAPS OF THE BATTLE FIELD MADE BY ACTUAL SURVEY, AND THE VARIOUS POSITIONS OF THE REGIMENTS AND ARTILLERY COMPANIES PLACED THEREON, WITH AN ACCOUNT OF THE MOVEMENTS OF EACH, PROCURED FROM THE COMMANDING OFFICER, OR AN OFFICER OF THE REGIMENT. ALSO,

AN ACCOUNT OF THE BATTLE.

ALSO, THE BATTLE GROUND OF THE 18TH JULY, 1861, WITH GENERAL BEAUREGARD'S REPORT OF SAID BATTLE.

By T. B. Warder & Jas. M. Catlett.

———•◦•———

RICHMOND:
ENQUIRER BOOK AND JOB PRESS.
TYLER, WISE, ALLEGRE AND SMITH.
1862.

PREFACE.

The object of this work is three-fold. In the first place it is designed to give the movements of the two armies in this great battle with such accuracy as to enable the professional reader to derive the instruction concerning the management of troops when engaged in battle that could not be gained otherwise except upon the battle field; and to become acquainted with the manœuvrings necessary to ensure success.

Secondly, to excite a spirit of patriotism throughout the country by attracting particular attention to the gallant bearing of our soldiers and their glorious achievements in the great battle. And, third, by enabling each soldier engaged in the battle, by recording his name on the page reserved for the purpose, and stating the number of his regiment, to have his movements in the fight fully explained; and the friend of any soldier, whether he survived the battle or fell in the deadly conflict, to obtain and preserve a record of his movements on that eventful and memorable day.

THE BATTLE OF YOUNG'S BRANCH, OR MANASSAS PLAIN,

Fought July 21, 1861.

After the entire exhaustion of all the means in the power of the slaveholding States to preserve to themselves an honorable peace, they find themselves involved in war. The only condition upon which war could have been evaded by them involved the unconditional surrender of their sovereignty and the sacrifice of all the rights and privileges guaranteed to them by the Constitution of their fathers. Could they have preserved peace and evaded war by the sacrifice of these, (humiliating, indeed, the thought) it would have been but transient; and the short and delusive interval would have been employed to strengthen the arm of oppression and increase its exactions—whilst tame acquiescence, on our part, would have sunk us in our own estimation, stifled the inborn spirit of our fathers, and rendered resistance more difficult, success more hopeless, and made peace to us but another term for vassalage.

It is because we are determined to be free, the alternative of war has been forced upon us. The issue has been joined. The God of Battles has been appealed to; and the struggle for freedom is begun.

The great battle, that unerringly tests the relative capacities of the two powers to sustain themselves in the unnatural conflict has been fought, and we derive therefrom the comfortable assurance that the result of this battle clearly indicates the result of the war.

It is not contended that there will be no more battles—many have since been fought with like results—or, that there will be no more so extensive and so bloody; but, *it is contended*, that the Battle of Young's Branch, or Manassas Plain, has produced such feeling throughout the two sections as must almost inevitably result in the final triumph of the Confederate States—a feeling of misgiving that greatly intimidates the North, while an increased confidence stimulates the South to a more invincible determination to prosecute the defence. It has proven that the Federals do not think they are contending for anything worth dying for; and, that the Confederates know they are fighting for everything dear to a free people, and would prefer death to defeat. And, what is best of all, it has proven to both North and South that the Lord is on our side.

In the war with Mexico, the battle of Buena Vista produced like results to those claimed for this battle. In every subsequent conflict between the two armies the Mexicans seem to have been overwhelmed with the conviction of their inferiority—a conviction that seldom fails to defeat an army before the fight begins. Since the battle of the 21st of July, no

Federal army can be brought into the field which is not already defeated by a misgiving that results from a consciousness of the superior valor and bravery of the Confederate troops, and the vastly superior skill of our Generals. For this reason, we must not expect to bring them into another battle with us, unless this consciousness is overcome by assurance of very superior advantage in some way or other—either in position or numbers. This battle has not only accomplished these important considerations, but it is very properly considered the greatest and most scientific battle ever fought on the American Continent. It is a matter of general interest, therefore, to know, as accurately as possible, the manner in which it was conducted.

In order to understand fully the movements of the troops of both armies, a survey has been made and the topography of the ground on which the fighting was done, accurately shown, and a general map showing the routes by which the two armies marched to the battle ground, that the reader may have no difficulty in understanding their movements and fully appreciating the skill by which they were conducted.

The Federals resorted to war to enforce their authority over the Confederate States, relying upon superior advantages and superior numbers to coerce us into ignoble submission to them. They boasted a population greater than that of the entire South, in the ratio of at least three to two, and the possession of all the means for military operations, both by land

and sea, that previously belonged to both sections. Having boldly proclaimed their purpose, the first object to be attained was the triumphal march of a grand army through Virginia to Richmond, and thereby to obtain possession of the Confederate Capital. The point from which this grand army was to march was Washington city; and the route by which it was to march, the Orange and Alexandria and Central Railroads. After this vaunting and audacious declaration of their purpose, their failure to move onward, under circumstances of so much advantage, could be attributed to nothing but sheer cowardice. They could not now be otherwise than fully conscious that the eyes of the world were upon them, and that upon their first battle depended, to a great extent, the success of all their efforts to accomplish their wicked designs upon the South, and they accordingly made the most ample preparations for the grand movement. An army sufficient in numbers, an abundance of the very best artillery, together with everything to render the movement effectual that science and ingenuity could suggest and supply, were all procured and placed at the command of one of the greatest and most scientific Generals of the age—General McDowell. This is stated in reference to General McDowell without the fear of contradiction; and his plans of operation in this one battle are relied upon to sustain the assumption, in the estimation of men of judgment, without reference to preceding circumstances which secured to him the high and responsible post.

While this movement was engaging the utmost exertion and skill of the Federals, the unpretending genius of the Confederate officers was employed to baffle and thwart it.

While the Federals were glorying in their extensive means, having all the army and naval preparations of the former United States, carefully provided in their palmiest days, the Confederates were reduced to circumstances which rendered their situation critical and embarrassing beyond conception—being cut off from all foreign ports and confined to means only within their own limits, with all the important forts and arsenals therein in the hands of the enemy. It is much doubted whether a nation ever was driven to the alternative of war with so great a disparity of munitions.

Gen. G. T. Beauregard was appointed to conduct this defensive movement along the Potomac. His sagacity soon led him to select Manassas Junction as the centre of his operations. Perceiving clearly the grand army from Washington could not proceed well towards Richmond, without securing the use of the Railroad, by which to forward its supplies, he at once addressed himself to the ample fortification of this place, so as to be able to hold it with the small force at his command against great odds. His force, at first very small, was also undisciplined. And to work them upon the fortifications, conflicted very much with their preparation for service in the field. To obviate this, he called upon the citizens of the surrounding country, for hands to work on the fortifications, and thereby was enabled to relieve the soldiers to considerable extent, and afford them opportunity for drilling. Companies, regiments and brigades arrived at this point with encouraging rapidity; some with arms and many without them. Where arms and ammunition were obtained for many of the men, the writer has not yet learned; for having been at Manassas, four days before the battle, he saw within the camp, companies of men for whom arms had not yet been procured.

About this time it was understood that Colonel Patterson, who was in command of a strong division of the Federal army, in the vicinity of Martinsburg, high up on the Potomac, had suddenly withdrawn from that point, in the direction of Washington, as if to join McDowell. (This was afterwards understood to be the fact, in relation to his movement, and Patterson was severely censured by the Federal press, for not being present with his command in this battle).

Gen. Johnston, who was in command of the Confederate army at Winchester, and who was watching the movements of Patterson, and trying to bring him to a fight, was too sagacious not to perceive at once the object of his secret withdrawal, and immediately took steps to counteract any effect produced by a junction of his forces with McDowell's, by ordering his command at once to Manassas, in aid of Gen. Beauregard.

Gen. Johnston, therefore, and a portion of his command, had arrived at Manassas before this battle, but a portion were detained on the route, by a collision of trains on the road.

Thus stood affairs as the grand army of the Federals was making demonstrations in the direction of Manassas.

Attention is now directed to the general map which exhibits Manassas—the road from this place to Centreville, by Mitchell's Ford—and Bull Run, from Sudley to McLean's Ford. This much of the country is considered enough for the object in view. All else, for prudential reasons, being designedly omitted.

Gen. McDowell's first plan was, to march on Manassas, either by Mitchell's and Blackburn's Fords, or the crossings below them.

Gen. Beauregard, with peculiar astuteness, had ascertained this, and prepared to make his passage of this stream, at any of these points, as difficult as possible, and to contest his progress over every inch of ground, from any point or points, at which he might effect a crossing, to Manassas.

Slight reconnoissances and small demonstrations satisfied McDowell he was anticipated, and caused him to change his plan. His demonstration on Mitchell's and Blackburn's Fords on the 18th, three days before this battle, was subsequent to the purpose to change his plan, and must, therefore, have been a deception, to induce Gen. Beauregard to believe his design was to make his strong effort to effect a crossing at these fords, and thereby induce him to concentrate the main body of his troops at these points, whilst he (McDowell) would effect a crossing higher up the stream.

The abandonment of his first purpose, and the adoption of his second, evinces, in Gen. McDowell, much that constitutes the great General, and entitles him to all that is claimed for him in this sketch.

His second plan was as follows:

The fifth division of his grand army, composed of at least four brigades, under command of Gen. Miles, was to remain at Centreville, in reserve, and to make a false attack on Blackburn's and Mitchell's Fords, and thereby deceive Gen. Beauregard as to his intention. The first division, composed of at least three brigades, commanded by Gen. Tyler, was to take position at the Stone Bridge, and feign an attack upon that point. The third division, composed of at least three brigades, commanded by Heintzelman, was to proceed as quietly as possible to the Red House Ford, and there remain, until the troops guarding that ford should be cleared away. The second division, composed of three or four brigades, commanded by Hunter, was to march, unobserved by the Confederate troops, to Sudley, and there cross over the Run and move down the stream to the Red House Ford, and clear away any troops that might be guarding that point, when he was to be joined by the third or Heintzelman's division. Together, these two divisions were to charge upon, and drive away, any troops that might be stationed at the Stone Bridge, when Tyler's division was to cross over and join them, and thus produce a junction of three formidable divisions of the grand army across the Run, for offensive operations against the forces of Gen. Beauregard, which he expected to find scattered along the Run for seven or eight miles—the bulk of them being at and below Mitchell's Ford, and so situated as to render a concerted movement by them utterly impracticable.

The merest glance at this plan of McDowell, wholly unknown to Gen. Beauregard, makes one almost tremble for the fate of his little army, and makes it difficult to realize that he could, and did, perceive it in time to thwart it.

All the information in relation to McDowell's plan and movements, is derived from the official reports of himself and officers. By these we also learn that each division of the grand army was well supplied with fine cavalry companies and an abundance of the finest artillery ever taken upon the field; that his grand army was to be in motion at 2 o'clock, A. M., of the 21st, and en route for their different positions in time to reach them and be in position by the break of day. Also, that they had four days rations cooked and stored away in their haversacks—evidently for the purpose of gaining

Manassas, and holding it, until their supplies should reach them by the railroad from Alexandria. Thus stood the arrangements and plans of the grand army on the evening preceding the battle of the 21st.

As before stated, General Beauregard had been anticipating his march on Manassas by the lower routes from Washington and Alexandria in that direction, and had previously learned from his movements that such was certainly his purpose. But that he had abandoned this plan and resolved upon turning his left flank by the plan above stated, he must have been wholly ignorant, as it was but a few hours before the battle that General McDowell communicated this to his most trusty officers. This appears from Barnard's official report. General Beauregard was, therefore, compelled to await the development of his plans by his movements on the morning of the battle. And had he not known the unholy designs of the Federals upon the South, which clearly indicated a defiance of God and contempt for His holy commandments, there would have been religious service in nearly all his camps, and his men allowed to rest, both from the duties of the camps and the turmoils of the battle on that holy Sabbath, selected by an infidel foe, for an attack upon a Christian people.

In his entire ignorance of the enemy's plan of attack, General Beauregard was compelled to keep his army posted along the stream for some eight or ten miles, while his wily adversary intended to develope his purpose to him by concentrating those formidable divisions of his army in rear of his left flank before the morning sun should unveil a single movement. And still under the impression that McDowell intended to march by the lower fords, he kept the principal body of his troops below and near Manassas. But in order to prevent a surprise, by a change of the enemy's plans, he took the precaution to deploy a portion of his troops in the direction of Sudley.

Colonel Robert T. Preston, in command of the 28th Virginia Regiment, was sent on picket duty in the direction of Cub Run Bridge. Colonel J. B. Strange, in command of the 19th Virginia Regiment, was stationed at Lewis's Ford. Colonel Eppa Hunton, in command of the 8th, and Colonel William Smith, in command of the 49th Virginia Regiments, were on the Lewis Hill, in proximity to the two fords—Lewis's and Ball's. Colonel J. B. E. Sloan, in command of the 4th South Carolina Regiment, and Major Wheat, in command of a Battalion of Louisiana Volunteers, with Latham's Battery, all commanded by Colonel Evans, were stationed on the Vanpelt Hill, commanding the Stone Bridge, and two companies of the 2d Mississippi Regiment were deployed as pickets in the direction of Sudley. These were the relative positions of the two armies on the morning of the 21st July, 1861.

Attention is now directed to the map of the battle field.

Before 2 o'clock, A. M., the grand army was aroused and ordered to be ready to march at that hour. It was, however, much regretted by General McDowell and some of his officers that the road at Centreville was so blocked up by the vast columns of his troops as to delay their forward movement until the Sunday morning sun developed to the Confederate Generals the direction of their march. Hunter's Division, which was to have been at Sudley by the break of day, did not get there until half-past nine. Tyler's, which was to have been at the Stone Bridge before day and quietly awaiting day break to make a feint upon the troops at that point, so as to hold their attention until Hunter should attack them in their rear, did not reach that point until half-past six. Heintzelman's Division, which was to reach the Red House Ford by day break, found no road leading in that direction, and followed Hunter on to Sudley and reached that point at eleven.

On ascertaining that the enemy was marching to his left, General Beauregard despatched Generals Bee and Bartow, with their respective commands, in the direction of Sudley quite early in the morning.

Colonel Robert T. Preston withdrew his regiment from the vicinity of Cub Run, where he had been stationed the preceding night, to Ball's Ford, to guard that crossing. Cannonading and skirmishing commenced quite early in the morning. Two of the enemy's batteries opened on Mitchell's and Blackburn's Fords, and two upon the Stone Bridge and Lewis's Ford, sending all kinds of deadly missiles at the men on guard at those places. For the purpose of ascertaining the point on which the enemy designed marching his main force, General Beauregard had given orders to his men to keep concealed at the several points, and not to return his fire until he arrived within a certain distance, except at Lewis's Ford, where two guns of Latham's Battery and two of Rogers's took position and returned his fire quite early in the morning.

From the top of the Vanpelt Hill, Colonel Evans observed Hunter's Division marching in the direction of Sudley, between eight and nine o'clock, with evident intention of flanking him, whereupon he withdrew his force from the Vanpelt Hill, after deploying three companies to protect the bridge, and took position at the Pittsylvania House; from which position he could protect both the Red House Ford and the Stone Bridge. By this time the commands of Generals Bee and Bartow had arrived at the Lewis Farm, and slight skirmishing announced the arrival of Hunter in the direction of Sudley.

General Beauregard was now compelled to resort to means to check him until he could ascertain his force and still further development of his purpose, it not being yet certain upon what point the enemy would direct the bulk of his army.

Of the commands of Bee and Bartow, the 4th Alabama, commanded by Colonel Jones, the 8th Georgia, by Colonel Gardner, the 2d Mississippi, commanded by Colonel Falkner, were ordered to march toward the Matthews House, and the balance of these brigades ordered to the Sudley Road in the direction of the Henry and Stone Houses. The two guns of Latham's battery were ordered, one to a position North of the Turnpike Road, opposite the Robinson House, and the other to a point on a hill North of the Stone House, near the point of the nearest woods, to said house. Imboden's Battery took position to the right and North of the Henry House, and two pieces of the Washington battery to the right of Imboden's. Colonel Evans threw the 4th South Carolina and Major Wheat's Battalion near the Sudley Road and Southwest of the Matthews House. The Regiments of Bee and Bartow's commands, with the 4th Alabama in front, had not quite reached the Matthews House when Hunter, with at least two Brigades of his Division, made his appearance in line of battle on the hill just above the Matthews House. A fierce engagement immediately ensued; the 4th Alabama, 8th Georgia, 4th South Carolina, and 2d Mississippi Regiments, and Wheat's Battalion, being the whole of the Confederate Infantry in the engagement, against at least two of Hunter's Brigades at first, soon joined by the balance of his Division, making the disparity of forces in favor of the enemy at least four or five to one, the disparity of artillery in his favor being still greater. Yet this little band of men stood their ground without yielding an inch for more than an hour against such tremendous odds. And though volley after volley of leaden hail was poured upon them, they wavered not, but stood as a wall of adamant, until Heintzelman appeared upon their left, and two Brigades of Tyler's Division, who had found the Red House Ford unguarded, and crossed over and taken possession of the Pittsylvania Hill, on their right, made it necessary, in order to avoid being entirely cut off, to fall back, which they did, leaving many of their gallant comrades killed and wounded behind them. Among these were Colonel Gardner, Colonel Jones and Major Wheat, all supposed to be mortally wounded. Their retreat was exceedingly awful. They fell back in the direction of the Robinson House under the fires of Heintzelman's Division on one side, Keyes' and Sherman's Brigades of Tyler's Division on the other, and Hunter's Division in their rear, and were compelled to engage the enemy at several points on their retreat, losing both officers and men, in order to keep them from closing in around them. Had they not been equal to the best regulars the world ever saw, no man of them could have been rallied afterwards. But with few exceptions they preserved good order, and by hard skirmishing stayed the flanking columns of the enemy, made good their retreat and formed again into line of battle immediately in the rear of the Robinson Hill, and did valuable service on other parts of the field.

This retreat on the part of our troops, under circumstances that would have driven the enemy in consternation from the field, as the sequel will abundantly prove, seems to have inspired him with the idea that he had obtained a glorious victory, and of course his troops were greatly encouraged by the anticipation of an easy march on Manassas. His purpose was now fully comprehended by General Beauregard, who at once despatched couriers below for as many troops as could be spared with impunity from those points. General Jackson's Brigade had been ordered to the battle field hours before from near Manassas, and was now hard by, but Earley's and Elzey's Brigades and Withers's, Kershaw's and Cash's Regiments, now just ordered, were not expected for some hours, and the now exultant enemy must be again checked if possible until their arrival. It was now about noon. Sherman marched his Brigade to the right and formed a junction with Hunter's Division, which, together with Heintzelman's Division, was proceeding to our left, pushing their artillery forward to more advanced positions, while Tyler, with Keyes' Brigade, remained upon our right on Young's Branch. In the meantime General Beauregard had ordered Captain Stanard's Battery of four guns to take position nearly East of the Henry House, Captain Imboden to fall back to the same position, five guns of the Washington Battery, two of Rogers's Battery and three guns of Pendleton's Battery to the same position, and Alburtis's Battery of four guns, with one gun of Pendleton's Battery, to the right of these, just in rear of an opening in the woods commanding the Robinson Hill. All except these last five guns commanded the various hills

West and Northwest of their position. Colonel Hampton's Legion, the 7th Georgia Regiment, commanded by Colonel Gartrell, and the 5th Virginia of Jackson's Brigade, commanded by Colonel Harper, and the 4th South Carolina, Colonel Sloan, were placed in position on the Robinson Hill. The other four Regiments of Jackson's Brigade were placed in position to support the batteries before named as follows: The 4th Virginia, Colonel James F. Preston, just in rear of the batteries; the 27th Virginia, Colonel Echols, to Preston's rear right; the 2d Virginia, Colonel Allen, to Preston's left; the 33d Virginia, Colonel Cummings, to Allen's left; the 49th Virginia, Colonel Smith, to Cummings' left; the 8th Virginia, Colonel Hunton, in rear of these; Colonels Strange and Robert T. Preston, with Latham's Battery, still protecting Lewis's and Ball's Fords. These were the several positions of the Regiments and artillery companies then on the field; and when the deadly conflict was a second time renewed, the fight on the left of the troops thus stationed was confined to the artillery principally for some hours, the enemy's infantry being much retarded in their advance movement by the incessant shower of iron hail and bombs that was poured upon them by our cannon. This compelled him to make his way to our left under cover of hills and ravines, and the washed places in the road. His artillery, however, was all the time returning a most destructive fire upon our lines and batteries, and the regiments on the Robinson Hill being in full view of it, suffered severely. These men remained firmly in position waiting the approach of the enemy's infantry to within reach of their guns. Tyler at length ordered Keyes' Brigade to ascend the Robinson Hill for the purpose of driving these men away and capturing the batteries in their rear. This was a grand idea if it could only have been accomplished; but no sooner did his columns advance within reach of the guns of those upon the hill, than they received a fire that caused them to hide in the ravines and shelter themselves in every conceivable way from the deadly missiles profusely dealt upon them. These brave men unflinchingly stood their ground, firing at every Yankee that dared to show his head, until they were ordered out of the way of the enemy's artillery that had been for some time pouring a destructive fire upon them. When they were observed to fall back, Keyes ordered his men to rush to their abandoned position on the hill, and, according to his own account, he held it but for a moment, for scarcely had he reached the Robinson House before the artillery of Alburtis and Pendleton were let loose upon him, and, without tardiness or seeming reluctance, he scampered back to Young's Branch.

It is hardly necessary to pursue the movements of this large portion of the enemy further, as they do not claim to have attempted another charge upon any part of our lines during the day. According to their own statement, they marched in very good order and in very gallant style, to the cover of the hills on Bull Run, claiming only to have cleared away the companies left in the morning at the Stone Bridge.

This, however, is but a pretext for their cowardly inactivity; for the company belonging to Wheat's battalion, (the Tigers), had left the Stone Bridge in the morning, time enough to be in the engagement with Hunter, at the Matthews House; Kilpatrick's company, of the 4th South Carolina Regiment, had left some time before, and joined the Hampton Legion prior to the fight at the Robinson House, and was among the foremost in driving them from that charge. And Captain Anderson's company, of the 4th South Carolina, the only remaining infantry company stationed at the Bridge, had left that post, and, joining the 49th Virginia Regiment, was led by Col. Smith to the extreme left of our line; whilst the two guns of Rogers's artillery, which had taken position early in the morning, on the Vanpelt Hill, commanding the Stone Bridge, had exhausted their ammunition sometime before, upon the batteries of Carlisle and Ayres, and retired to another position. It will be perceived, therefore, that this gallant brigade of Federals found no troops of any description about the Stone Bridge to clear away.

This gallant brigade, formidable alone for its imposing appearance as to numbers, was seen by some of the Confederate officers, who mistook their innocent design to shelter themselves by seeking a position under cover of the bluffs of Bull Run, for a purpose to menace our right, and gave them needless annoyance by sending a few cannon balls among them, which they acknowledge kept them as quiet as mice, and in constant look out for the best chances of escape in the dire ction of Washington. The fear and alarm that characterized them may be readily inferred from their imagination, that they were compelled to retreat from the Robinson Hill, to avoid being cut to pieces by a galling fire from behind *breastworks!* Keyes states his loss in killed, wounded and *missing,* at 242, much the larger portion of which were the missing. And when it is considered there was no real occasion for the slightest disorder among the men, we can easily form a proper estimate of their character as soldiers.

During this time, the divisions of Heintzelman and Hunter, with Sherman's Brigade, had been working themselves along the routes best protected from the fire of our artillery, to the left. They had managed to get forward several of their batteries; that commanded by Ricketts having taken position South of the Henry House, while their columns of infantry were in. formidable array along the road from the Stone House to the woods South of the Henry House —along a branch that lies a little West of the road, diverging from it slightly to the West of South—along Young's Branch, South of the Dogan House—and under cover of all the hills on Dogan's farm, and others in that direction; all being kept in temporary check by the volleys of shot and shell poured upon them by the artillery East of the Henry House. Reinforcements from the direction of Manassas were now being expected, when the enemy could be engaged at all points, though with unequal force.

The enemy having attempted to silence our batteries, by a charge made by Keyes' Brigade, as before stated, and failing most signally, now attempted to accomplish this by a charge upon the left. For this purpose a regiment was ordered to charge from the right of Ricketts's Battery, through the small pines lying to the left of the Confederate batteries. In this charge, the regiment or regiments making it, came in contact with the 49th Virginia Regiment, occupying the extreme left of our line; whereupon, without waiting for orders, the 49th returned the charge, causing them to beat an instantaneous retreat in the direction of the Sudley Road, and pursuing them, drove them from the battery of Ricketts and captured the guns. On getting possession of the battery, they remained and fired from the wheels of the cannon, resting their muskets upon them, for a short time, but finding the enemy very strong beyond this point, and the nearest of them occupying the Sudley Road, which was worn into a ravine or gully, affording them an almost impregnable position, they fell back to the pines beyond the hill. Seeing them fall back, the enemy again advanced forward, and again attempted, under cover of the pines, to the left of our battery, to charge upon and silence it.

They hardly gained the pines, before they came in contact with Col. Cummings's and four companies of Col. Allen's regiments, which resolutely repelled the charge, and drove them back to their position in the road. They reached also, Ricketts's Battery, re-capturing it. But, finding the enemy completely protected by the road, and themselves exposed to a most destructive fire, they also fell back to the pines. The enemy now made a more general forward movement. He pushed columns of his men to the top of the Henry Hill, literally covering it from the woods South of the house to its base near the Stone House, while the woods and pines were swarming with the red and blue jacket Zouave and Chasseur. It had now become a matter of considerable importance to him to hold the Henry Hill. Much of his artillery in position on the hill, had had the teams killed by which it was drawn, and, consequently, could not be taken away. It was necessary, therefore, to hold the hill in order to hold the batteries which had been already twice captured. It was evident that overwhelming numbers were to be repelled or the position abandoned, which Gen. Beauregard was so anxious to hold until the arrival of his reinforcements.

Gens. Bee and Bartow again threw their commands in front of his heavy columns—the 7th and 8th Georgia regiments, the 2d Mississippi and 4th

Alabama Regiments, with the 4th South Carolina and the Hampton Legion; Col. Fisher leading up the 6th North Carolina Regiment on the extreme left of these—all except the 6th North Carolina having been engaged once or twice before during the day. Upon these devolved the herculean task of holding many times their numbers back until the earnestly looked-for reinforcements came. The conflict soon became awfully terrific. The roar of musketry was incessant. The enemy now believing that to fall back again would turn the battle against him, became more obstinate. The Confederates, with unyielding and unwavering determination, pressed upon him. Bartow falls—Bee falls—still they press on—Fisher falls, but his men charge the more furiously. Gartrell and Falkner are wounded, but falter not; all evidently trying to bring it to a hand to hand fight—to a charge of bayonets. This is too close for the Yankees; they begin to fall back to the hill-side toward the road.

At this moment the desired reinforcements arrive. Colonels Jas. Preston, Echols, Harper, Hunton, Withers and Strange join the charge across the Henry Hill, while Gen. Smith, who arrives from the cars, Colonels Kershaw and Cash charge directly from the South and along the Sudley Road, a part of Kershaw's regiment occupying the road and charging the enemy that are protecting themselves by its banks. The charge is now pushed with increased spirit and with indomitable perseverance. They fall back to the road, which is almost impregnable, but now becomes too hot for them. Our soldiers press steadily upon them; they fire spiritedly; but seemingly unconscious of danger, our lines advance. They abandon the road and take to the ravine beyond; a hot fire pursues them and they gain the top of the hill in their rear, where they are met by the reserve from Young's Branch, who had been under the shelter of the hill for some hours, and here they resolve to make another stand. Kemper now places his artillery on the West side of the Henry Hill. The Newtown Artillery commanded by Capt. Beckham, which had been for some time in position East of the Chinn House, firing upon the advancing enemy wherever he could be seen in the direction of Sudley, and contributing much to his annoyance, now changed position to the top of the hill, commanding a good view of the hill to which he had retreated. All the regiments in the last charge at the Henry House were continuing a galling fire upon him from the road. Col. Robt. T. Preston, commanding the 28th Virginia Regiment, took position to the left of Cash's position in the wood; Gen. Elzey's brigade, composed of the Baltimore, (Colonel Elzey), 10th Virginia, Col. Gibbon, and ———— regiments took position to Preston's left and near the foot of the hill. Gen. Early's Brigade, composed of the 24th Virginia, 7th Virginia, (Col. Kemper,) and 7th Louisiana, (Col. Hays) Regiment, took position near Chinn's Spring, on the extreme left, and perhaps some other Confederate troops were on the ground. Of this, however, the writer is unadvised.

Thus were the two armies posted when the last conflict took place between them, and upon which depended the enemy's last hope of victory. His whole columns were now engaged and soon began to give way in confusion. They fell back from the top of the hill to the thickets in their rear, and to Young's Branch, and finding themselves hotly pursued, they broke ranks and fled in all directions, each one seeming mindful of his own safety and perfectly regardless of the safety of the rest, whilst all seemed actuated by the old saying, of "Devil take the hindmost."

So soon as their columns began to give way, Capt. Beckham instantly changed his position to a hill on Young's Branch in the direction of Groveton, and contributed much to facilitate their flight, while Capt. Kemper turned two, and others four more, of their own long-ranged guns, captured on the Henry Hill upon them, increasing much their fright and the velocity of their speed. Elzey's and Earley's Brigades and a number of regiments started in the pursuit, also, Beckham's and Kemper's Batteries. All pursuit by the infantry was soon found to be vain, except to prove the Federals are far better at running than they are at fighting.

A few of the shots from Beckham's artillery overtook them as they passed the Pittsylvania House, but they were soon protected by the hill which they descended towards Bull Run at much more than " double quick."

Capt. Kemper was more successful. Taking the Turnpike Road he was able to get in sight of a large number of them as they were passing the Spindle House, and by a single shot, which he sent ahead to invigorate them by the assurance of his immediate presence in their rear, he smashed one of their cannon, killed three men and two horses.

The scampering among them at this point became at once so great as to make another shot unnecessary. He again pursued them to within range of Cub Run Bridge and sent ahead numerous missiles upon most deadly errands, of the effects of which, an eye witness thus speaks:

[Extract from Burnside's Official Report.]

"Upon the bridge crossing Cub Run, a shot took effect upon the horses of a team that was crossing. The wagon was overturned directly in the centre of the bridge and the passage was completely obstructed. The enemy continued to play his artillery upon the train carriages, ambulances and artillery wagons that filled the road, and these were reduced to ruins. The artillery could not possibly pass, and five pieces of the Rhode Island battery, which had been safely brought off the field, were lost."

The scenes that here ensued beggar all description. The wildest confusion prevailed. Cannons and caissons, ambulances and train wagons, with the horses attached, and hundreds of soldiers, all fleeing with the utmost speed, alarmed and terrified, rushed helter skelter down the hill into a common heap. Those upon horses dismounted; those who had taken to the wagons and ambulances for conveyance, jumped out, while those on foot, joined in the common scramble to cross the stream and get away from their pursuers. Here much of the valuable fruits of this unprecedented victory was gathered.

There were many of the Confederate forces of whom no mention is made in the foregoing part of this narrative, who are entitled to as much credit as if they had been in the hottest of the battle. Under the circumstances controlling the disposition of the Confederate troops, Gen. Beauregard was compelled to station them at all the crossings of Bull Run, not knowing at which the enemy was determined to pass. And though he was enabled, on the morning of the 21st to ascertain his purpose to turn his left flank, yet he could not be certain but that his design was to cross a large force at any point from which the troops might be withdrawn. Hence the necessity of keeping his troops posted at all the fords throughout the whole day. McDowell kept the troops stationed at each ford, continually mindful of his presence, by the thundering of his cannon, the whistling of balls and explosion of shells immediately among and around them, for nearly the whole day. Our true hearted boys not being allowed to return his fire, were thereby placed in a far more unpleasant situation than the battlefield, and no wonder that we hear so many complaining of not being allowed to participate in the conflict of the field, for they were being constantly killed and wounded without the satisfaction which retaliation affords.

These men were as much participants in the glorious events of the 21st, as if they had been in the struggles of the Matthews, the Robinson or the Henry House, and they ought to content themselves with the assurance, that, stationed as our troops were, it depended on Gen. McDowell as to which of them should be in the hottest of the fight.

Had he adhered to his first purpose, and sought to cross Bull Run at Mitchell's and Blackburn's Ford, or still lower down, then the hardest of the fighting would have been by the troops stationed at those places; whilst those stationed at the upper fords would have been comparatively inactive. Nor were the troops below, inactive on the 21st. They had the enemy in their sight pouring destructive and death-dealing missiles upon them in ceaseless showers until late in the day, when they showed themselves by a determined charge upon them. But the invading hosts, true to their instincts, and with characteristic cowardice, fled precipitately, leaving their pursuers far in the rear.

It is much to be regretted that none of the gallant movements of the Confederate Cavalry on this memorable day can be given. Their ceaseless activity on all parts of the field, and constant presence at all points suited to their operations, has rendered it impossible to do them even partial justice, and has caused the effort to do so to be wholly abandoned. It is but just, however, to say that in perusing the enemy's reports, we find them at all points terribly annoyed by our cavalry, and constantly engaged in repelling their desperate charges; and, when the rout began, the impetuosity with which they dashed into the enemy's retreating columns, is already a matter of history.

It has been stated that General McDowell, the leader of the Federal army, displayed a very high order of generalship in this battle. This has been done to show that truth and justice to all are the aim of the author, and that ample justice can be done to the veriest enemy who is lending his skill and abilities, which eminently qualify for high distinction if exerted in a just and righteous cause, to the destruction of everything sacred to freemen, but who, by wanton misdirection of both, is doomed to reap ignomy and die disgraced and unlamented. But to estimate properly the military skill and ability of the brave and sagacious, yet unpretending Beauregard, who, with so much apparent ease, completely baffled all his well and adroitly laid plans, is no easy task.

The plans of McDowell and the movements by which they were most signally thwarted, are now before the reader. The result is almost incredible. And, when we consider the advantages of the one side and the disadvantages of the other, and that superior numbers were on the side of the superior advantages, the result of the conflict is rendered marvelous beyond conception, and places General Beauregard far above his competitor, and at once ranks him among the greatest warriors of the world. How thankful the people of the Confederate States should be to an Allwise and Beneficent Providence that such a man has been given us to direct our defence against the wicked designs toward us of so tyrannical, fanatical and unprincipled, and, at the same time, so formidable a foe as that with which we have to contend. How much it should add to our gratitude to reflect, that while we have one leader who has, at the very commencement of the struggle, attained high pre-eminence over the leaders of the enemy, we may have in our midst many who may not only be his equals, but who, when similar circumstances shall develope their abilities, shall prove to be superior to him. We will be thankful that we have one such as General Beauregard, and, believing, as we do, that he is sent of God to enable us to meet successfully our present unprecedented emergency, we can trust our cause into his hands and ask God's blessings upon it and him. Yet, who can doubt, that when the war shall be ended, it will be impossible to decide which of our officers has displayed most ability, or which of our soldiers most bravery.

Let it not be forgotten too that Gen. Johnston was upon the battlefield, whose mere presence is sure guaranty of victory, and who only awaits the opportunity to develope sagacity, skill and power, that shall call forth and command the admiration of the world. But, above all things, let us never be unmindful that "salvation is of the Lord;" that it is He who gives wisdom to the officer and courage to the soldier; who makes great men for great emergencies, and with whom alone are the issues of the battle. Let us praise Him that he has recognized our cause; that He has manifested His favor and His protection thus far in the struggle, and, with grateful hearts, implore a continuance of His favor upon us and upon our arms until we obtain a glorious and permanent peace.

FOURTH ALABAMA REGIMENT—COLONEL JONES.

The Fourth Alabama Regiment, Colonel Jones, passed up Bull Run to the right of the Lewis House, crossed the Turnpike and advanced to within one hundred and fifty yards of the Matthews House, where they met the advancing forces of the enemy. They were discovered emerging from the woods and on the hill in the direction of Sudley. A severe engagement took place at this point, and, after the repulse of four regiments of the enemy (as stated in their official report) this regiment, being overpowered by superior numbers, retreated through a small body of woods, crossed Young's Branch about two hundred yards below the Stone House, passed the the Robinson House, and formed in a ravine in the rear thereof. The enemy's shells, fired at the Hampton Legion and the Seventh Georgia Regiment, who were posted on the lane between the Robinson House and the Turnpike, falling and exploding among them, caused a further retreat through the woods to the open land in the direction of the Lewis House, where they halted until Brigadier General Bee led them by a left flank movement to the spot where he fell. Finding themselves a second time without a commander, and the men suffering for water, they retired to a branch near Lewis's House to quench their thirst; after resting a short time, drew up in a line and remained there, supposing the enemy to be advancing. President Davis arriving and proposing to lead them, they started back for the scene of action. A messenger arriving, informed them that the enemy were in full retreat. A further advance was deemed unnecessary, and they returned to Manassas at 11 o'clock P. M. The Regiment suffered severely, both in the engagement and retreat. Their gallant Colonel [Jones) fell mortally wounded, and was captured by the enemy. Lieutenant Colonel Law was disabled by a ball which shattered his left arm at the elbow. Also, Major Scott was wounded and many other officers and men. The loss of this regiment was very great.

SECOND MISSISSIPPI REGIMENT—COL. W. C. FALKNER.

This Regiment left their place of bivouac on Bull Run in the vicinity of Mitchell's Ford, on the morning of the 21st July, and marched in the direction of Stone Bridge, heavy firing being heard from that quarter. Arriving near the Turnpike, they ascertained the position of the enemy's flanking columns, and took position near the corner of the woods, in the rear or North of the Stone House. Immediately after forming into line, a heavy fire was opened upon them from one of the enemy's batteries, posted upon the rising ground in Dogan's field and to the West of Sudley Road. They replied with telling effect, judging from the confusion produced in the enemy's ranks, and a great number of them must have been killed and wounded. The regiment held its position for more than an hour, exposed to the fire of artillery and infantry. By order of General Bee, two companies of this regiment, one under Capt. Buchanan and the other under Capt. Miller, were sent forward as skirmishers in the direction of Sudley. They did their work well, pouring a galling fire into the enemy as he advanced. Their own loss was considerable; many being killed and wounded. Seeing heavy columns of the enemy advancing by a flanking movement to the left, and towards the position occupied by Capt. Imboden's battery near the Henry House, and supposing that corps in danger of being surrounded and captured, the regiment moved by the left flank, and took position in rear of and for the support of Captain Imboden, who, appreciating the danger of his position, marched his battery to one of greater security. The enemy making demonstration in overwhelming numbers, both of artillery and infantry, upon the road leading to Manassas and to the South of the Henry House, the position of the regiment was again changed to a point near that road, and near a piece of woods, distant from the Henry House about three hundred yards. Here the enemy had posted his battery, the different sections of which extended along the ridge nearly parallel with the woods. This regiment, in conjunction with others, now opened fire, killing the men and horses and capturing what proved to be the battery commanded by Ricketts. The struggle at this point was of the most sanguinary character, and decided the fate of the day. The men were engaged in combat at the very mouths of the cannon, and gallantly and successfully contested every inch of ground. Col. Falkner received a severe, though not mortal wound, after having had his horse twice shot under him. Of the officers, Lieutenants Brossellman, Smith, Butler, and Palmer, and seventy-nine privates, were killed, and many mortally wounded.

ELEVENTH MISSISSIPPI REGIMENT—COLONEL ———.

Owing to some delay in their transportation by

railroad from Winchester, only two companies of this regiment took part in the engagement of this memorable day, and these formed part of the Second Mississippi Regiment, whose brilliant achievements are stated above.

EIGHTH GEORGIA VOLUNTEERS—COLONEL WILLIAM M. GARDNER.

This Regiment marched early in the morning from a point below on Bull Run, in the direction of the Lewis House, to the road to Ball's Ford, thence to the Ford and formed in line of battle, where they remained a short time; then marched to a point near the Henry House and drew up in line of battle again. The enemy having exhibited his front near the Matthews House, they again marched by the Henry House, crossed the turnpike road East of the ford of Young's Branch, below the Stone House, down the East side of said branch a short distance, crossed and marched over a hill West of a drain and some pine thickets to a point at the extreme North margin of a piece of pine near the Matthews House, and here formed in line of battle to support the 4th Alabama Regiment, fighting to the left of this position on their arrival. Here they immediately engaged the enemy, who had advanced to the Matthews House, and ice house, and East and West of this house. The engagement was fierce and terrific, and lasted near an hour. General Bartow's horse was killed here, and Colonel Gardner was badly wounded.

From this point they fell back nearly on the line by which they advanced, skirmishing with the enemy, who were seeking to cut them off at several points, and, recrossing Young's Branch, marched up the hill in direction of the Robinson House and formed a junction with the 7th Georgia Regiment, at the turnpike, just east of the Robinson Gate. Here they fired at the advancing columns of the enemy, which had now reached the branch. They then marched to the lower side of a small clump of pines near the road, and nearly up the drain to near the point at which General Bartow fell, where they made a resolute charge on the enemy about the Henry House and succeeded in driving them again from their batteries. From this point they retired to the branch East of the Lewis House and remained there all night. It is very easy for one, at whatever distance he may have been from the scene of strife, to see the hardships endured and privations suffered by this regiment, when we consider the impossibility of procuring food or water during the whole of the day, to say nothing of the exposure to wounds and death at every step on their march.

FOURTH SOUTH CAROLINA REGIMENT—COLONEL J. B. T. SLOAN.

This regiment formed in line of battle Sunday morning at 4 or 5 o'clock on a hill near Vanpelt's House, and remained until half-past 8 o'clock, A. M. They left two companies to guard the Stone Bridge and changed position to a point near the Pittsylvania House, with Wheat's Battalion on their right and two guns of Latham's Battery in front. They had not more than formed before they discovered the enemy were still flanking them, and moved immediately, throwing themselves in front of the enemy (marching from the direction of Sudley) taking position with their left on the Sudley Road, and their right resting in the woods to the rear of the Stone House; one of Latham's guns and Captain Terry's Cavalry on their right. They here opened fire on the advancing enemy. The enemy gaining a position which gave them considerable advantage, they found it necessary to advance through the woods, and took position on the North side of the woods and much in a line with the North margin, with General Bee's command on their right. Here they stood a severe fire from the enemy in their front and along the road, which damaged them very much, killing and wounding some fifty of their men. They were ordered to fall back to a point of wood North of the turnpike road and a short distance to the East of the gate leading into the Robinson House, and there drew up again in line of battle and fought the enemy, who had now advanced to near Young's Branch. From this position they fell back again, to avoid being flanked by the enemy, to the drain below the Robinson House, formed and returned in line of battle to the house. Here they were ordered to lie down and await the nearer approach of the enemy, now advancing from the direction of the Stone House, and just below on Young's Branch. Being soon rallied by Colonel Evans, they here fought under a terrific fire of the enemy near in their front for some time, and were ordered back to the opening East of the wood that skirts the drain to their rear. From this point they marched to and took position nearly East of the Henry House, and with Hampton's Legion on their left, charged upon the enemy around the Henry House, driving them back, and thence to Ricketts' Battery, pulling out three of their guns; Lieutenant T. J. Sloan acting as captain to one, Ferguson loading, and fired on the retreating enemy near the Sudley Road beyond the Stone House. Then they moved the guns two hundred yards to a point commanding the approach to Vanpelt's House, and were ready to fire when General Beauregard and Governor Manning commanded them to take the guns off to the Lewis House. They carried them some distance in that direction and left them until morning. Captain Anderson, with his company, belonging to this regiment, who was left in the morning near the Stone Bridge to guard this point, in the afternoon marched across the mouth of Young's Branch and joined a battalion commanded by Colonel Smith, of Virginia, and was placed with this battalion on the extreme left of our line, and made the first infantry charge upon the Ricketts' Battery, which they captured.

The other company of this regiment, which was left in defence of the Stone Bridge, was commanded by Captain Kilpatrick, and joined the Hampton Legion just before the engagement with the enemy at the Robinson House, and fought with the Legion both at the Robinson and the Henry House. These two companies left the bridge on seeing the Federal Army move up the Run with evident intention to cross some where above and flank them—the regiment having gone from their support and engaged the enemy at the Matthews House. They, thereupon, connected themselves with the nearest regiments and moved promptly into action, doing good service and manifesting the patriotic spirit and determined fortitude which characterized the great body of the Confederate troops engaged in this great battle.

MAJOR WHEAT'S BATTALION—LOUISIANA VOLUNTEERS.

This battalion camped the night of the 20th July in an orchard back of Vanpelt's House, marched in the morning about 8 o'clock to the Pittsylvania House, and then drew up in line of battle with the 4th South Carolina Regiment and two of the guns of Latham's Battery; but finding the enemy were marching around by the ford at Sudley, they left their position at the Pittsylvania House and marched in direction of Dogan's to the Sudley Road and formed in line of battle near the road and North of the woods back of the Stone House, and here, in conjunction with several other regiments before named, stood the enemy's first charge, keeping him in check for some time. These men suffered very much, many of them being killed and wounded, and Major Wheat himself receiving what was supposed at the time a mortal wound, but as if spared by a kind Providence for a good and noble purpose, he speedily recovered. After Major Wheat had fallen, Captain Harris took command, and on receiving orders to that effect, fell back to the bridge across Young's Branch. The Rifle Tigers, which belong to this battalion, were deployed in the morning early to a point on Bull Run, above the Stone Bridge, where it was thought the enemy's infantry and cavalry might be able to cross, from which point they opened the fight of the 21st with the enemy's pickets at 7 o'clock, A. M. But hearing a brisk fire in the direction of Sudley, and observing the enemy move in that direction, they marched directly to the Matthews House, and while passing between the enemy and this house, with a view to take a sheltered position, Adrian received a shot from the enemy, wounding him slightly. They, however, gained the desired position, and gave the enemy much trouble, killing an officer and many of his men before they were compelled to abandon their position to him. They then fell back, having sustained much loss, and charged him again in conjunction with the 4th Alabama Regiment. In this second charge they advanced from the foot of the hill near the woods back of the Stone House to a point near the top of the hill, and not far from Matthews' House, from behind which the enemy was sending deadly missiles at the Alabamians. From this point their fire upon the enemy was sharp and destructive.

SEVENTH GEORGIA VOLUNTEERS—COLONEL L. J. GARTRELL.

This Regiment left Manassas between 6 and 7, A. M., and took their first position between the Henry House and the Sudley Road about 10, A. M. The enemy not having reached this point, but now marching in heavy column towards the Robinson House, they marched to that house and took their second position between it and the Turnpike Road about an hour after. On attaining this position, they found the enemy now not in reach of their guns, and lay down to shelter themselves as much as possible from the showers of ball and shell from the enemy's cannon, during which time a number of the men were killed, and Col. Gartrell's horse knocked from under him by the explosion of a shell. This position being too much exposed, and the enemy not coming in reach of their guns, they changed their position to the Turnpike Road, East of Robinson's Gate, which is the nearest point of the road to the house; from this point they fired on the enemy while crossing Young's Branch, and charging up the hill towards them; then they changed their position to the rear of a clump of pines and upon or near a small branch lying nearest to and East of the Robinson House;

then fell back through an opening in the wood lying East of said branch and took a position just East of the wood. From this position they marched to a point East of the Henry House and East of General Bartow's column, and charged on the enemy, now occupying the ridge on which the house stands, and with other regiments drove the enemy from this ridge and captured a portion of their battery, planting our colours upon it by E. W. Hoyle, Sergeant Newman, and others; maintaining the position about an hour until the enemy fled. These men were under the fire of the enemy's artillery or infantry all day, and of 580 men, lost in killed and wounded 170. In this last engagement, Colonel Gartrell was wounded and Henry C. Gartrell, his son, killed, and General Bartow killed also. They returned to their camp at Manassas, arriving there about 9 o'clock at night, having endured for fourteen or fifteen hours the toil and fatigue of the march and of the battle field, amid clouds of dust and smoke, without water or food.

HAMPTON'S LEGION.

The first position of Colonel Hampton's men known to the writer was between the Robinson House and the Turnpike Road, where they took a prominent part in checking the advance of the enemy, charging in that direction. In this position they stood a long time exposed to the deadly fire of the enemy's artillery while waiting the arrival of his infantry to a point within reach of their guns; during which time many of them were killed and wounded. Keyes' Brigade of Tyler's Division made a charge upon them with a view to drive them back and capture the battery in their rear, which was holding in check nearly all the rest of the enemy's forces. A spirited contest ensued, the enemy keeping as much as possible under cover of the hills, while the artillery continued to play upon them. They were finally ordered to fall back, which they did in good order, taking position in rear of the nearest woods to the East of the Robinson House. From this point they marched several hundred yards and took position to the East of the Henry House, and charged upon the enemy now occupying the Henry House. They were here engaged in an almost hand to hand fight with the heavy columns of the enemy, who were struggling to maintain the possession of this hill and their batteries, which had been placed upon it. They succeeded, however, in conjunction with other regiments, in driving them back and holding the hill and the captured battery until the general rout of the enemy. They then marched in pursuit of them to Cub Run Bridge, aiding in the capture of a large number of cannon, wagons, muskets, prisoners and ambulances, and many other articles too tedious to mention, until a very late hour at night.

FIFTH VIRGINIA VOLUNTEERS—COLONEL KENTON HARPER.

This regiment took position in an opening in a

wood to the rear of the Robinson House, East of a drain running to the bridge across Young's Branch, East of said house and in front of Alburtis's battery, about 12 M.; then marched to the house and engaged the enemy advancing in that direction from the Stone House; then fell back to the rear of wood to right of their first position, and also to the right of the position now occupied by the 7th Georgia. From this position they advanced and took position Northeast of the Henry House, charged upon the enemy in the direction of the Stone House, passing down a ravine running in that direction nearly to the Turnpike Road under a heavy fire from the enemy, causing him (the enemy) to fall back; then returned to last position and charged with 4th and 27th Regiments to the road. Lieutenant Paxton here placed the flag of the 7th Georgia Regiment on the guns here taken.

FOURTH VIRGINIA REGIMENT—COLONEL JAMES F. PRESTON.

This regiment marched from near Manassas by Lewis's House and took position just at the West margin of pines in sight of the Henry House, about 12, M. Artillery companies just in front of them. They lay here under fire of the enemy's guns directed at the artillery in their front, their balls whistling and their bombs exploding in their midst for two-and-a-half hours; many of the men being killed and wounded, (Gen. Beauregard's horse being killed by enemy's cannon, just in front of this regiment, and just in rear of fifth gun from the left of artillery) during the occupation of this position, yet not a man moved. The enemy having been repeatedly driven back from the hill about the Henry House, were now struggling in an almost hand to hand fight to regain and hold it, and the artillery upon it, when the artillery in their front was ordered back, and they wheeled to the left and charged just to the left of the Henry House, driving the enemy from the road by a reckless and furious charge, to some distance from the house, and captured six of their guns at the road below the house, which they held and turned upon their retreating columns.

TWENTY-SEVENTH VIRGINIA—COLONEL ECHOLS.

This regiment took their first position just in the rear right of Col. Jas. F. Preston's, above described, and left their position at the same time, marching and charging to his right, leaving the Henry House to their left, charging the enemy along the road and beyond, capturing, at the road, the flag of the first Michigan regiment.

SECOND VIRGINIA—COL. J. W. ALLEN.

The position of this regiment, at first, was a little to the left of Col. Preston's in the pines, from which position they charged with the 33d Virginia regiment in the direction of that section of Ricketts' battery farthest South. On reaching the guns, being in a very exposed position, they fell back.

THIRTY-THIRD VIRGINIA VOLUNTEERS—COL. A. C. CUMMING.

This regiment took its first position in the pines, immediately to the left of the 2d Virginia regiment, Col. Allen, and charged the enemy, who were seeking to avail themselves of the pines to the left of our artillery, in order to silence and capture it. They drove them back in the direction of the two sections of Ricketts' battery farthest to the left, driving them from the guns, when they found from their exposure to a terrific fire from the enemy occupying the road, it was best to fall back, which they did, over many of their own men, who had fallen in the desperate and unequal conflict, and a far greater number of the enemy whom they had slain.

FORTY-NINTH VIRGINIA REGIMENT—COLONEL WILLIAM SMITH.

This regiment bivouacked on the Lewis Farm, on the night of the 20th. Early on the morning of the 21st it took position a little above the Lewis Ford, just at the mouth of Young's Branch. This position it maintained, without firing a gun, until early in the afternoon, when it was ordered to march towards the Henry House, and take position on the extreme left of our line which was directly in front of the Rickett's battery. Scarcely had they taken position, before they were charged upon by the enemy's flanking column. They immediately returned the charge by a shout, a rush forward, and a well directed fire, driving their assailants before them. They moved forward for two hundred yards, when the smoke and dust excluded the sight of all surrounding objects. They were halted until this should clear away, throwing themselves in the meantime upon the ground, and loading and firing at will. When the dust and smoke cleared away a little, they found themselves within fifty steps of the Ricketts' Battery, which they charged upon immediately and captured. They stood awhile among the artillery, many of the men resting their guns upon the cannon wheels, as they fired, for some minutes, when it was ascertained the enemy were ensconced in the road, which was much washed out, the banks of which afforded them perfect protection against their foe: and they fell back, with a loss in killed and wounded of one-fourth of their men. This was the first charge made by any of our infantry upon this battery; but from a description of its condition given by these men, when they reached it, there was evident proof of a previous charge upon it by the cavalry, which had killed enough of their horses and cannoniers to prevent its removal or operation with much success.

TWENTY-EIGHTH REGIMENT VIRGINIA VOLUNTEERS—
COLONEL ROBERT F. PRESTON.

This regiment was thrown out as skirmishers on the night of the 20th towards Cub Run Bridge, and early on the morning of the 21st returned, and crossing Bull Run a few hundred yards below Ball's Ford, marched up to and took possession of said Ford at six o'clock, A. M. They remained there until two or two-and-a-half, P. M. They then advanced, passing North of the Lewis House and along the road that leads up a drain from the Lewis to the Henry House, to a point in the rear of the nearest oak wood South of the latter house, then crossed the drain to left and took position in the edge of the woods about half-past three o'clock. Here they met and repulsed the first Michigan regiment, and captured Col. Wilcox, Capt. Withrington and two privates, and relieved Capt. Kemper, who had been captured by some Chasseurs or Zouaves, (see Kemper's incident); then passed along, leaving the wood to the right and some scattering cedars to the left, to the Sudley Road, filed out into the wood left of the road and marched to the top of the hill, where the enemy had taken position on the opposite side of Young's Branch from the Dogan House, thence to the Henry House; and marched in pursuit of the enemy, passing by the Stone House to the woods and cornfield beyond, on the Sudley Road. The enemy being far in advance of them, they returned to the Turnpike Road, by the Robinson Gate, along the road to the Stone Bridge; thence to Lewis's House and to camp back of Weir's House near Manassas. The mysterious appearance of this regiment at Ball's Ford, very much embarrassed the movement of Schenck's brigade in that direction. In passing near the Lewis

House, Col. Preston met many carrying off the wounded, very much discouraged, and who gave him a most deplorable account of the state of affairs on the battle ground, informing him that we were whipped, and only one of them all, gave him reason to hope for victory.

He hurried on his men, and to his astonishment found the enemy's lines breaking up and going away in all directions, when he arrived in sight of them. At the request of Col. Preston, the following note is made:

Wm. P. Douthat, of the County of Botetourt, with Frederick Noel, Ferdinand Painter, Charles Kemper, Owen Watson and ——— Watson, came to this regiment on the morning of the 21st and fought through the whole engagement.

NINETEENTH VIRGINIA VOLUNTEERS—COLONEL J. B. STRANGE.

This regiment, on the morning of the 21st, was stationed at Lewis's Ford, where the company officers had thrown up breastworks during the two preceding days and nights, under orders to lie in the trenches and keep concealed, and not to fire unless the enemy came within one hundred yards. Soon after sunrise, the enemy's skirmishers came in sight, in the bottom on the other side; and from the pines and oakwood beyond they fired at them from their Parrott guns every missile that could be fired for the space of three hours, both from their cannon and skirmishers, but none of them coming within the distance above named, they did not return their fire until the enemy withdrew, and then they were ordered about three o'clock, P. M., (all except Capt. Duke's Company from Albemarle, who was left to hold the Ford,) to advance upon the field. Passing near the Lewis House they marched under a heavy fire from the enemy (not aimed at them, as they were not in sight) to the branch, in the direction of the Henry House. The balls were now falling so thick around them, they were ordered to lie down awhile. They then advanced into the fight just about the turn of the battle, and pursued the enemy across by the Pittsylvania House; across Bull Run, by the the Ford beyond said House, and then up the Run to Sudley; recrossing the run at Sudley, they marched along the road to the Stone House, thence through the battle ground to their post in the morning, bringing with them many prisoners. These men deserve as much credit for maintaining their position at Lewis's Ford, under the fire of the enemy, according to orders given them, as though they had been in the hottest of the battle. It was of exceeding importance to the success of our forces, that the division of the enemy stationed near that Ford, should be prevented from crossing, which they were essaying all the morning to do, and which would have thrown them on the rear of our line of battle.

EIGHTH VIRGINIA—COLONEL EPPA HUNTON.

This regiment bivouacked on the Lewis farm the

preceding night, and took position on the morning of the 21st, by a strip of wood skirting a small branch running along the West side of the Lewis Hill and emptying into Bull Run above the Lewis Ford and within a few yards of the mouth of Young's Branch. From this position it was held in readiness to march at a moment's notice, to the support of the regiments stationed at Ball's or Lewis's Fords, should the enemy attempt to cross at either of those places.

The enemy having withdrawn from those fords, Col. Hunton marched his regiment directly into the fight, drew them up into line immediately in front of the enemy occupying the Henry Hill, and charged with other regiments engaged, directly towards the Henry House, driving the enemy from his position on the hill, back into the road; continuing the charge, passing on either side of the Henry House, until the enemy were completely routed and fled in all directions. The coolness, courage and bravery evinced by these men, is worthy of all praise, and is a sure guaranty that in all future conflicts with the enemy, they will secure fresh laurels and an increased portion of their country's gratitude.

SECOND SOUTH CAROLINA REGIMENT.

This regiment received orders to march from a point, three miles distant from Lewis's House, on Bull Run, about 12 M., to the support of General Jackson's brigade, which was then engaged in the battle. They left the Lewis House to their right in their line of march, and formed in line of battle in rear of the woods to the East of the Henry House; then marched to the Sudley Road, and formed on the road, the left occupying the road, and charged along the road, which had been a safe harbor for the enemy for some time. This charge was so destructive that he quickly fled to the hill West of the road, when he again rallied his forces in great numbers. This regiment immediately wheeled into the road, which afforded the men much protection from the leaden shower now poured upon them, and held their position against fearful odds, until all the available forces on the field, and expected to arrive, got into position, engaging the whole of the enemy's line, and produced the universal rout of his vast columns. This regiment then pressed forward in the pursuit along the Turnpike Road, to the bridge over Cub Run, from which point they were ordered back to the Stone Bridge, where they bivouacked all night.

Colonel Cash's regiment marched and fought in conjunction with Colonel Kershaw's throughout the day, and it is deemed unnecessary to make a note of his movements, except to say that he marched into battle on his left, and that on reaching Cub Run he remained with his regiment, aiding in securing the valuable capture of men, artillery, arms, wagons, ambulances, provisions, &c., &c., until one o'clock on the morning of the 22d.

EIGHTEENTH VIRGINIA REGIMENT—COLONEL ROBERT E. WITHERS.

This regiment marched from Camp Walker near Manassas, arriving at Lewis's House at about one o'clock, P. M., and drew up in line of battle and marched in line directly to the Henry House; was ordered to halt awhile about half way, in rear of the pines East, then marched forward again just through the pines; found themselves immediately in rear of other regiments and halted fifteen to twenty-five minutes, and from three to four o'clock charged the enemy, who occupied both sides of the road leading from Sudley to Manassas. They maintained their ground until the enemy retreated beyond the hill towards Dogan's, took a battery of six rifled pieces, from which the enemy had been driven several times before, and some strange officer turned two of them upon the retreating enemy. They continued a short distance in pursuit, then marched through the battle ground South of the Turnpike Road, crossing Bull Run a short distance below the Stone Bridge, and took position on the road East of the bridge, for the purpose of cutting off the enemy's retreat, but finding the enemy had already passed that point, and were some distance ahead of them, they returned to Camp Walker.

THE SIXTH NORTH CAROLINA STATE TROOPS—COLONEL FISHER,

Arrived at Manassas on the morning of the 21st,

hurried by forced march to the battle field; passed the Lewis House, and, by a direct route, reached a position near the head of a small drain, just to the left of this drain in the woods, the most Southern section of Ricketts' battery in their front. Here they met the advancing columns of the enemy's right flank, consisting of infantry and artillery, which soon engaged their special attention, and, in co-operation with other regiments, they eventually succeeded in capturing the battery. The gallantry and courage displayed by these troops on that occasion are worthy of all praise; none showed signs of fear, but each vied with the other to assist in securing the prize. At each volley of their musketry the enemy bit the dust, and, at last, no longer able to withstand the onslaught, fled precipitately from the field. The heroic Colonel Fisher fell, shot through the head, and died immediately. Lieutenant Mangum was also mortally wounded, near the spot where his Colonel fell. The regiment suffered severely, both in officers and men.

GENERAL ELZEY'S BRIGADE, COMPOSED OF THE TENTH VIRGINIA REGIMENT, COL. S. B. GIBBONS, THE BALTIMORE REGIMENT AND —— REGIMENT.

The regiments of this brigade having marched together and acted in conjunction throughout the 21st, it is thought best not detach them in this notice of their movements. They marched from Manassas early in the afternoon of the 21st, and took their first position, sometime in the afternoon, in rear of the woods, South of the Henry House, intending to charge through the woods towards the house, but finding other regiments charging in that direction and the enemy falling back to the hill between the Chinn and Dogan House, they marched through the woods lying West of the Sudley Road, and charged them, advancing in the charge over the hill, and through the brush on the opposite side of the hill to Young's Branch. On reaching this branch the enemy were fleeing rapidly across by Dogan's House and over the surrounding hills. They reached Young's Branch about four o'clock, and returned to the Henry House, where they met President Davis. They pursued the enemy to the Stone Bridge, expecting them to seek the Turnpike about that place, but seeing nothing of them they returned to Manassas the same night.

GEN. (THEN COL.) J. A. EARLY'S BRIGADE, COMPOSED OF THE TWENTY-FOURTH VIRGINIA, COL. EARLY; SEVENTH VIRGINIA, COL. KEMPER, AND SEVENTH LOUISIANA, COL. HAYES.

The regiments of this brigade marched and acted in conjunction all day. They were stationed, on the morning of the 21st, near McLean's Ford, which is about one and-a-half miles below Blackburn's Ford, on Bull Run. From this point they marched to the battle ground, by no road, but through the fields, which contributed no little to the fatigue of the march, passing South of the Lewis house, and North of Conrad's house, leaving the wood West of the Sudley Road just to their right, and took a position at Chinn's Spring not far from Chinn's House. They here engaged the enemy who occupied the hill between them and the Dogan House. The enemy quickly retreated to the wood and pines that stood on the Northwest side of said hill, skirting Young's Branch. Advancing upon them here, they quickly retreated in great confusion, and in all practical directions. They pursued them, passing a little West of the Dogan House, by the Matthews' house and Pittsylvania House, to the ford below, and there bivouacked all night. Having performed this marvellous day's work, these men reposed, necessarily, upon empty stomachs all night, not knowing but that before the morning, they would be compelled to resist the passage of heavy columns of the enemy. But knowing certainly that they would have to march some 7 or 8 miles next morning, at least, before they could relieve their hunger.

CAPT. PHILIP B. STANNARD'S BATTERY—FOUR GUNS.

This battery arrived at the Junction, from Winchester, late in the evening of the 20th July, and remained near Mitchell's Ford that night, and was ordered early on the morning of the 21st to Lewis's House and there divided into two sections—two guns taking a position not ascertained, for a short time, and then joined the other two, which had marched to a point indicated on the map, and commenced firing on the enemy in the direction of the Dogan, the Henry and the Robinson Houses, who were marching in heavy columns towards and to the West of the Henry House, and here continued firing in conjunction with other batteries for many hours, keeping the enemy in check, and greatly impairing the effectiveness of his batteries until their design was fully understood, and arrangements made for their defeat. They were then ordered to retire to the Lewis House, and fire upon the enemy as they retreated. Their ammunition being well nigh exhausted (one of their caissons having exploded during the engagement) but two of the guns were used for this purpose, from the hill near the Lewis House, in direction of Vanpelt's, to which the enemy responded from a high point in the Turnpike Road near Vanpelt's, killing Lieut. Edgar Macon. The service rendered by this battery is incalculable.

CAPT. A. L. ROGERS' BATTERY—FOUR GUNS.

Two of the guns took position, commanded by Lieut. Henry Heaton on a hill near the mouth of Young's Branch and commenced firing on the enemy early in the morning, who had taken position in the woods over the Run and at the distance of five or six hundred yards from Lewis's Ford, and opened a most destructive fire on the infantry placed here for the protection of the Ford. These two guns maintained this position until early in the afternoon, when the enemy ceased firing and withdrew. They then took position with the batteries East of the Henry House, and continued until all were ordered off the field. The other two guns, commanded by Capt. Rogers, took position near the road and on the point of the hill where the road passes Vanpelt's, commanding the Stone Bridge, and commenced firing about 10 o'clock, A. M. at the enemy, across the Stone Bridge, until their ammunition was exhausted, and then retired to the top of the hill, on the opposite side of Young's Branch.

CAPT. PENDLETON'S BATTERY—FOUR GUNS.

This battery took position East of the Henry House, along with the Washington Artillery, Stannard's and others, about half-past 12 M, and remained two-and-a-half hours there, then changed position to a hill Northwest of the Lewis House and fired at the enemy, who was retreating through the large body of woods, through which the Turnpike runs, and which lies about half-a-mile East of the Stone Bridge.

CAPT. ALCURTIS'S BATTERY.

This battery took its position East of an opening in the woods skirting a small branch running below the Robinson Hill, commanding the said hill, with one of Capt. Pendleton's guns, immediately on the right, and the other three of Pendleton's and several other batteries off a little to the left. On the appearance of the enemy on the Robinson Hill, this battery and the gun of Pendleton's battery on the right, opened a deadly fire upon them, and drove them, in much confusion and with considerable loss, to Young's Branch on the opposite side of the hill. They continued to operate with decided effect upon the enemy wherever visible from their position, for many hours—causing the entire brigade commanded by Keyes to retire from the fight altogether, and seek the shelter of the hills on Bull Run, and contributing with the batteries on their left, to hold in check, the overwhelming flanking columns of Heintzelman, Hunter and Sherman, until the Confederate infantry were in position to repel them, when they were ordered to other positions, in the rear, from which they did much destruction to the masses of retreating Federals, as they fled from the battlefield.

KEMPER'S BATTERY—FOUR GUNS.

Capt. D. Kemper received orders to march from Mitchell's Ford at one o'clock; passed Lewis's House, to the road leading from Sudley to Manassas, striking the road just back of the wood South of the Henry House—there left one gun commanding the road to Sudley, and took position with the other three on the right of the road about half-way between the road and Ricketts' battery, now finally captured at about half-past three, P. M. and fired 142 rounds on the enemy, who had retreated to the high hill West of the road—from which position the enemy was soon compelled to retreat. Capt. Kemper then laid hold of two of the guns of Ricketts' battery, which were of longer range than his own, and placed them in position, and used them upon the retreating enemy with dreadful effect. He then marched with his battery by the Robinson House and Turnpike Road, repeatedly placing his guns in position and sending deadly missiles ahead at columns of the enemy retreating before him, and when in reach of Cub Run Bridge, over which the enemy were passing in great numbers, he fired upon them; the first ball striking a team about half-way the bridge, upsetting the wagon in such a manner as perfectly to block up the bridge, and by a few well directed shots, made the whole scene about the bridge, in the language of the official report of one of the Federal officers—"a mass of ruins."

THE STAUNTON ARTILLERY, CAPT. J. D. IMBODEN.

This battery passed the Lewis House on the morning of the 21st July; hearing heavy firing in the direction of the Stone House, on the Turnpike Road, and supposing the enemy to have advanced beyond that point, took position on the ascent of the hill, after crossing the branch near the Lewis House. After ascertaining that the enemy had not advanced as far as he supposed, the battery was again put in motion, passing through a small corn field, and through an opening in the pines to a position to the North and right of the Henry House. Here the enemy's columns first came in view, and for nearly three hours a brisk engagement was kept up with batteries and upon open columns of the enemy in position and advancing upon the hill North of the Turnpike Road, and between the Dogan and the Matthews Houses; being unsupported by either artillery or infantry (save for a brief period by two pieces of the Washington Artillery), and the enemy advancing in heavy force, the battery was limbered up and fell back to a hill about four hundred yards distant and formed in line with the Washington, Leesburg, Stannard's and Pendleton's batteries; (one of the guns was disabled and lost during the last change of position). Firing was kept up about three quarters of an hour, when the ammunition becoming exhausted, the battery was compelled to retire from the fight.

CAPT. H. G. LATHAM'S BATTERY—FOUR GUNS.

Two of these guns, under command of Capt. Latham and Lieutenant Folks, were placed in position at Lewis's Ford, and opened fire on the enemy at 7 o'clock, (Schenck's brigade,) who had commenced firing upon the infantry at the Ford from the wood beyond. These are represented as the first guns that fired on the enemy—and maintained this position until about 2 o'clock, P. M., and then changed position to a hill in the rear of the ford, where they were joined by the other two guns which had taken position under command of Lieuts. Davison and

Leftwich, on a hill near the Turnpike road, commanding the Stone Bridge, on which point the enemy opened fire at 6 A. M., from the head of the field below the bridge and beyond the run; but having orders to remain concealed until the enemy came within canister range, they did not return their fire. The enemy not coming within canister range, they were ordered to change position to the point near the Pittsylvania House, about half-a-mile North of the Stone Bridge. After arriving at this position, they discovered the main body of the enemy had passed for the purpose of flanking our troops, and they were ordered to the Turnpike and marched up the road to Robinson's Gate, one gun taking position in the field and on a hill North of and not far from this gate, and fired upon the enemy approaching by the Sudley Road, the head of whose column appeared back of the Matthews House; the other passed on and took position on the hill in rear of the Stone House and near the road from Sudley, and fired on the enemy approaching across the hills to the right and left of the Sudley Road, and along that road; and, supported by several regiments of infantry, held them in check for more than an hour, and until they were reinforced by artillery, infantry and cavalry, which took position about five hundred yards in their rear. They then withdrew under the fire of ten of the enemy's guns and took position South of the Turnpike, on a hill side. From this position they opened again on the enemy's advancing column, until they obtained their last position with two guns. Then changed position to the right of batteries on the right, and maintained this last position until their ammunition was exhausted; they then withdrew and joined Latham; all four of the guns being now together at the position last taken by Latham, fired on the enemy to the left of Ball's Ford; then changed position to a point on the next hill West, and opened fire on Schenck, who was approaching the Stone Bridge, until he withdrew; then fired to left oblique upon a portion of the enemy who were moving from above towards the Bridge, under cover of the hill, and drove them back; continued firing from this point until the close of the fight, and upon the retreating enemy.

THE WASHINGTON ARTILLERY.

Two rifled pieces of this artillery took position on the morning of the 21st, to the right of North from the Henry House near Imboden's first position, about half-past nine o'clock, and fired for some time at the enemy as he first came in sight along the Sudley Road, until, discovering the enemy had got the range of their position, they changed it to a point a short distance off to their right and renewed the fire a short time in the same direction, and then fell back and joined three other guns of the battery which were all that had marched to the battlefield, and took position with other batteries nearly East of the Henry House, and fired at the enemy whenever he could be seen until half-past two to three P. M. and until all the batteries were ordered off the ground. Gen. Jackson then ordered one rifled piece to take position in the orchard North of the Lewis House and fire on the enemy as he retreated along the Turnpike East of the Stone Bridge. This battery being at the left of the batteries in position East of the Henry House received a heavy fire from the Brooklyn Chasseurs, from a point in the pines to their left.

FIFTH SOUTH CAROLINA REGIMENT—COL. M. JENKINS.

This regiment was one of three that composed the brigade of Gen. Jones, and was stationed on the morning of the 21st at McLean's Ford, and about three o'clock, P. M., Gen. Jones ordered his brigade over the Run to charge upon the enemy's position, which consisted of two brigades and some eight or ten pieces of artillery stationed near the woods on the road leading from Mitchell's and Blackburn's Fords to Centreville. The enemy stood the charge but a few minutes and fell back under the fire of Jones' brigade, and retreated hurriedly towards Centreville. Col. Jenkins's regiment occupying a very exposed position in the charge, suffered very severely for the short time they were engaged, losing about seventy-five men in killed and wounded within the space of five minutes.

11TH NORTH CAROLINA REGIMENT—COL. KIRKLAND.

This regiment was stationed with the other regiments of Gen. Bonham's brigade at Mitchell's Ford. They laid under the fire of the enemy until late in the day, when they left their trenches and pursued the enemy to within three quarters of a mile of Centreville, and were then thrown out in the direction of Cub Run Bridge, remaining in that vicinity all night, capturing many prisoners and other valuables of the enemy.

i

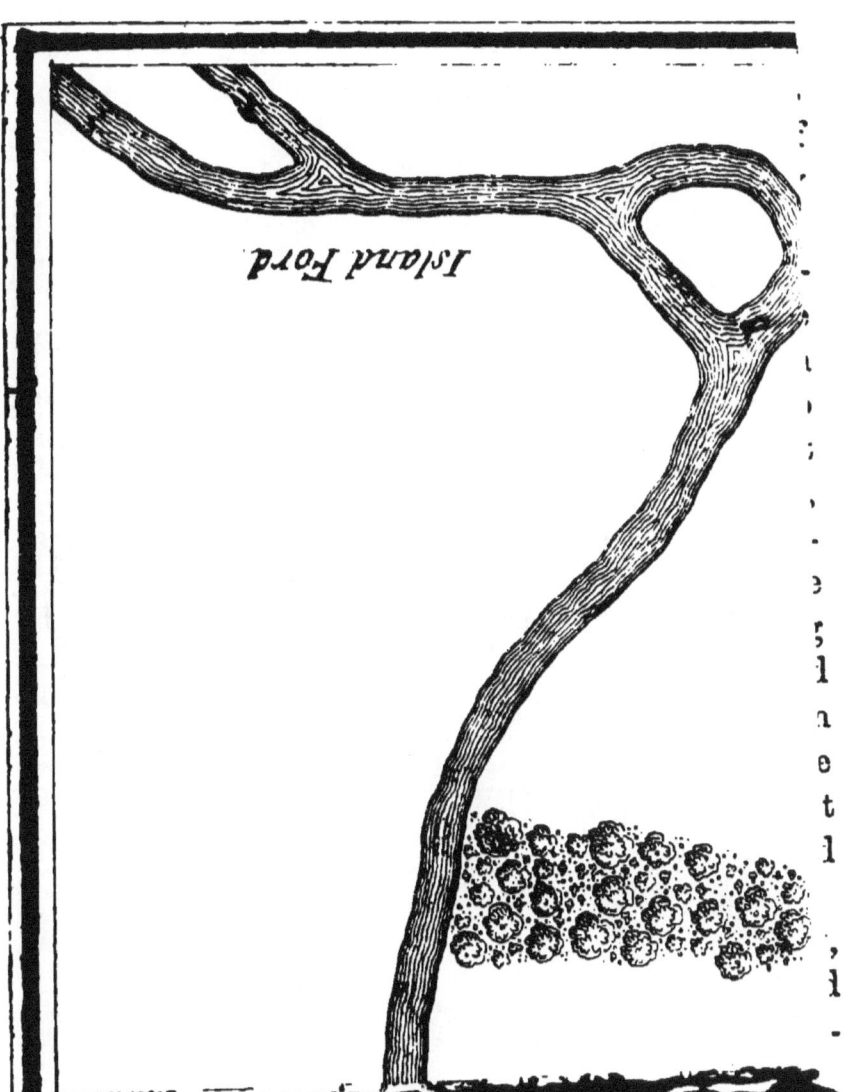

INCIDENTS.

There are many incidents of this battle that should be mentioned in connection with this account of it, but which are omitted because of the difficulty of doing exact justice in every case. There were three noble boys, of whose daring the writer has heard from sources reliable in his estimation, of which he will make a record, simply because they are mere boys.

A boy belonging to the Fourth Alabama Regiment, by the name of Oakley, whose parents reside near Huntsville, after the retreat was ordered from the Matthews House, remained a moment behind to do a kindness to a wounded comrade, who was shot in that desperate conflict, and was captured, and, after taking his musket from him, the enemy conducted him to the rear. The enemy soon became engaged again in a skirmish with our troops, during which Oakley picked his opportunity as he passed near some bushes, and seizing the musket of a fallen Yankee, ran into the bushes and got away. While seeking to join his regiment, he came in contact with a wounded Federal officer, and captured and conducted him safely to our lines.

Another boy, the son of William T. Early, Esq., near Charlottesville, Virginia, having received a military education, was employed to go to Manassas to drill the militia that had been ordered to that place. While there the battle of the 21st came off. That gallant young fellow shouldered his musket, walked to the battle ground, some six miles distant, there fell in with Colonel Smith's regiment and fought with them through a most desperate charge upon the enemy, and at one time went some distance in advance of the regiment, and concealing himself until a Federal officer rode forward and came near him, he fired upon him and made him bite the dust. The smoke of his gun drew the fire of a whole regiment, one ball striking his cap and another his wrist, inflicting a slight wound.

A third boy, named Elliot, of humble parents, of Fauquier county, Virginia, joined the Fauquier Guards against the earnest entreaties of his parents and friends, and after a gallant charge upon the enemy on the Henry Hill, and capturing the Battery of Ricketts, in retreating through the dense pines got separated from his company and came in contact with a Chasseur or Zouave, who had also got separated from his company, and the two with one accord engaged each other. Young Elliot proved the better man and left his antagonist weltering in his blood.

CAPTURE AND RELIEF OF CAPTAIN KEMPER.

Captain Delaware Kemper's artillery was attached on the 21st, to the command of Colonel Kershaw of

South Carolina, and marched with Col. Kershaw's command to the battle ground, when the battle was raging on the Henry Hill. Colonel Kershaw took position on the Sudley Road, just in rear of the skirt of woods South of the Henry House. Seeing no position for artillery, Kemper was ordered to remain South of the woods until Kershaw should drive the enemy out of the woods and secure a position for his artillery on the other side, from which he could play his artillery successfully upon the enemy. Kershaw found the woods full of Zouaves and Chasseurs, and made a furious charge upon them; whereupon, many of them fell killed and wounded and many unhurt. Kershaw's men passed over them, supposing them to be dead, but after passing them they arose and secreted themselves in some small cedars that stand just in the rear of the woods. Kemper now rode briskly to the front, and inquired of Kershaw if he could give him a position. Kershaw pointed him to a position, when he hurried back for his battery. In returning he passed through the small cedars which concealed the Chasseurs, and they suddenly arose all around him, and, pointing their guns at him, demanded his surrender. He saw no chance of escape and at once dismounted and called for an officer to take his sword. No officer being present, Kemper demanded that he should be taken to one, insisting on his right to surrender his sword into the hands of none but an officer. They replied, "we do not know where to find an officer." "Take me," said Kemper, "anywhere, I will go with you." In looking around they saw a regiment not far off, and one of them exclaimed, "there is a regiment of our men, let us take him to them." To this Kemper consented; and, on nearing this regiment they found it to be the Twenty-eighth Virginia. Ascertaining their mistake, they left their prisoner and ran for dear life. This timely rescue, as the reader has doubtless learned, resulted most fortunately to us, and most disastrously to the enemy.

AN INCIDENT

BY M. L. WHITTEN,

Chaplain of the Ninth Alabama Regiment.

Upon Virginia's sacred soil
  Two hostile armies met,
The one was struggling to be free
  From tyranny's foul net;

The other, to make his meshes strong,
  And bondage to complete,
To trample down the freeman's rights
  Beneath the tyrant's feet.

The battle hot and hotter grew,
  The leaden hail flew fast,
While many a foeman bit the ground
  And quickly breathed his last.

The tyrant's hosts in wild alarm
  Their footsteps backward trod
While freedom's sons with stalwart arm
  Pursued in strength of God.

By chance one spied a fallen foe
  The death shot in his frame,
The purple tide, now oozing out,
  Was quenching life's bright flame.

A kindly hand his wants supplied
  And cooled his heated brow.
"Will you," the dying foeman cried,
  "Before my God now bow,

And pray for me whose spirit soon
  Shall leave this earthly clod,
And, from this gory battlefield,
  Shall go to meet its God!"

With cheeks all red with burning shame,
  The kind one then did say,
"Although I blush to own the truth,
  I know not how to pray."

'Twas then upon his panting steed,
  In hot pursuit up rode,
A son of Old Dominion's soil,
  Who loved and served the Lord ;

And, at the dying foe's request,
  He bent the suppliant knee,
And raised his voice and heart to God,
  While Jesus was the plea.

And while his strains, in eloquence,
  Rang out upon the air,
And soared aloft, like incense sweet,
  To Him who heareth prayer,—

The dying foeman's face grew calm,
  His eye with love grew bright
For one, who but an hour ago
  He met in deadly fight.

He strove to clasp his feeble arms
  Around the suppliant's neck,
The effort far too feeble proved,
  Alas, they were too weak.

And when the warm and fervent prayer
  In simple faith had ceased
A smile remained upon the lip,
  The spirit was released.

The outstretched arms, too feebly raised,
  Were folded on his breast,
The stiffening limbs in order placed,
  The spirit was released.

With heart now warm with love divine,
  The hero onward sped,
Reflecting on that sunbright clime,
  Where no more blood is shed.

Longing to see the day arrive
  When war's sad notes shall cease,
And freemen's efforts shall be crowned
  By long continued peace.

GENERAL BEAUREGARD'S OFFICIAL REPORT OF THE BATTLE OF BULL RUN, ON THE 18th OF JULY, 1861.

HEADQUARTERS 1ST CORPS ARMY OF THE
POTOMAC, MANASSAS, August, 1861.

GENERAL: With the general results of the engagement between several brigades of my command and a considerable force of the enemy, in the vicinity of Mitchell's and Blackburn's Fords of Bull Run, on the 18th ultimo, you were made duly acquainted at the time by telegraph, but it is my place now to submit in detail the operations of that day.

Opportunely informed of the determination of the enemy to advance on Manassas, my advanced brigades, on the night of the 16th of July, were made aware from these headquarters of the impending movement, and in exact accordance with my instructions, a copy of which is appended, marked " A," their withdrawal within the lines of Bull Run was effected with complete success during the day and night of the 17th ultimo, in the face of, and in immediate proximity to, a largely superior force, despite a well planned, well executed effort to cut off the retreat of Bonham's Brigade—first at Germantown and subsequently at Centreville, whence he withdrew by my direction, after midnight, without collision, although enveloped on three sides by their lines. This movement had the intended effect of deceiving the enemy, as to my ulterior purposes, and led him to anticipate an unresisted passage of Bull Run.

As prescribed, in the first and second sections of the paper herewith, marked "A," on the morning of the 17th of July, my troops resting on Bull Run, from Union Mills Ford to the Stone Bridge, a distance of about eight miles, were posted as follows:

Ewell's Brigade occupied a position in vicinity of Union Mills Ford. It consisted of Rhodes's 5th and Seibel's 6th Regiments, of Alabama, and Seymour's 6th Regiment of Louisiana Volunteers, with four 12-pounder howitzers, of Walton's Battery, and Harrison's, Green's and Cabell's Companies of Virginia Cavalry.

D. R. Jones' Brigade was in position in rear of McLean's Ford, and consisted of Jenkins' 5th South Carolina, and Burt's 17th and Fetherstone's 18th Regiments of Mississippi Volunters, with two brass 6-pounder guns of Walton's Battery, and one company of Cavalry.

Longstreet's Brigade covered Blackburn's Ford, and consisted of Moore's First, Garland's Eleventh and Corse's Seventeenth Regiments Virginia Volunteers, with two 6-pounder brass guns of Walton's Battery.

Bonham's Brigade held the approaches to Mitchell's Ford; it was composed of Kershaw's 2d, Williams's 3d, Bacon's 7th and Cash's 8th Regiments South Carolina Volunteers; Shield's and Del. Kemper's Batteries, and Flood's, Radford's, Payne's, Ball's, Wickham's and Powell's Companies of Virginia Cavalry, under Colonel Radford.

Cocke's Brigade held the fords below and in vicinity of the Stone Bridge, and consisted of Withers's 18th, Lieutenant-Colonel Strange's 19th, and R. T. Preston's 28th Regiments, with Latham's Battery and one company of Cavalry, Virginia Volunteers.

Evans held my left flank and protected the Stone Bridge crossing, with Sloan's 4th Regiment South Carolina Volunteers, Wheat's Special Battalion, Louisiana Volunteers, four 6-pounder guns, and two companies of Virginia Cavalry.

Early's Brigade, consisting of Kemper's 7th, Early's 24th Regiment of Virginia Volunteers, Hays's 7th Regiment Louisiana Volunteers and three rifle pieces of Walton's Battery, Lieutenant Squires, at first were held in position in the rear of, and as a support to, Ewell's Brigade, until after the development of the enemy, in heavy offensive force, in front of Mitchell's and Blackburn's Fords, when it was placed in rear of, and nearly equi-distant between McLean's, Blackburn's and Mitchell's Fords.

Pending the development of the enemy's purpose, about ten (10) o'clock, A. M., I established my headquarters at a central point, McLean's farm house, near to McLean's and Blackburn's Fords, where two

6-pounders of Walton's Battery were in reserve; but subsequently, during the engagement, I took post to the left of my reserve.

Of the topographical features of the country thus occupied, it must suffice to say that Bull Run is a small stream, running, in this locality, nearly from West to East, to its confluence with the Occoquan River, about twelve miles from the Potomac, and draining a considerable scope of country, from its source in Bull Run Mountain, to within a short distance of the Potomac at Occoquan. At this season, habitually low and sluggish, it is, however, rapidly and frequently swollen by the summer rains until unfordable. The banks for the most part are rocky and steep, but abound in long used fords. The country on either side much broken and thickly-wooded, becomes gently rolling and open as it recedes from the stream. On the Northern side the ground is much the highest, and commands the other bank completely. Roads traverse and intersect the surrounding country in almost every direction. Finally, at Mitchell's Ford the stream is about equidistant between Centreville and Manassas, some six miles apart.

On the morning of the 18th, finding that the enemy was assuming a threatening attitude, in addition to the regiments whose positions have already been stated, I ordered up from Camp Pickens, as a reserve, in rear of Bonham's Brigade, the effective men of six companies of Kelly's Eighth Regiment

Louisiana Volunteers, and Kirkland's Eleventh Regiment North Carolina Volunteers, which having arrived the night before, en route for Winchester, I had halted, in view of the existing necessities of the service. Subsequently, the latter was placed in position to the left of Bonham's Brigade.

Appearing in heavy force in front of Bonham's position, the enemy, about meridian, opened fire with several 20-pounder rifle guns from a hill, over one and a-half miles from Bull Run. At the same time Kemper, supported by two companies of light infantry, occupied a ridge on the left of the Centreville Road, about six hundred yards in advance of the ford, with two 6-pounder (smooth) guns. At first the firing of the enemy was at random, but by half-past 12, P. M., he had obtained the range of our position, and poured into the brigade a shower of shot, but without injury to us in men, horses or guns. From the distance, however, our guns could not reply with effect, and we did not attempt it, patiently awaiting a more opportune moment.

Meanwhile, a light battery was pushed forward by the enemy, whereupon Kemper threw only six solid shot, with the effect of driving back both the battery and its supporting force. This is understood to have been Ayres's Battery, and the damage must have been considerable to have obliged such a retrograde movement on the part of that officer.

The purposes of Kemper's position having now been fully served, his pieces and support were withdrawn across Mitchell's Ford, to a point previously designated, and which commanded the direct approaches to the ford.

About half-past 11 o'clock, A. M., the enemy was discovered by the pickets of Longstreet's Brigade advancing in strong columns of infantry, with artillery and cavalry, on Blackburn's Ford.

At meridian the pickets fell back, silently, before the advancing fire across the ford, which—as well as the entire southern bank of the stream, for the whole front of Longstreet's Brigade—was covered at the water's edge by an extended line of skirmishers, while two 6-pounders of Walton's Battery, under Lieutenant Garnett, were advantageously placed to command the direct approach to the ford, but with orders to retire to the rear as soon as commanded by the enemy.

The northern bank of the stream, in front of Longstreet's position, rises with a steep slope at least fifty feet above the level of the water, leaving a narrow berme in front of the ford of some twenty yards. This ridge formed for them an admirable natural parapet, behind which they could, and did approach, under shelter, in heavy force, within less than one hundred yards of our skirmishers. The southern shore was almost a plain, raised but a few feet above the water for several hundred yards; then rising with a very gradual, gentle slope, and undulations, back to Manassas. On the immediate bank there was a fringe of trees, but with little, if any, undergrowth or shelter, while on the other shore there were timber and much thick brush and covering. The ground in rear of our skirmishers and occupied by our artillery, was an old field extending along the stream about one mile, and immediately back for about half a mile to a border or skirting of dense, second growth pines. The whole of this ground was commanded at all points by the ridge occupied by the enemy's musketry, as was also the country to the rear, for a distance much beyond the range of twenty pounder rifled guns, by the range of hills on which their batteries were planted, and which, it may be further noted, commanded also all our approaches from this direction to the three threatened fords.

Before advancing his infantry the enemy maintained a fire of rifle artillery from the batteries just mentioned for half an hour, then he pushed forward a column of over 3,000 infantry to the assault, with such a weight of numbers as to be repelled with difficulty by the comparative small force of not more than twelve hundred bayonets, with which Brigadier General Longstreet met him with characteristic vigor and intrepidity. Our troops engaged at this time were the First and Seventeenth, and four companies of the Eleventh Regiment Virginia Volunteers; their resistance was resolute, and maintained with a steadiness worthy of all praise; it was successful, and the enemy was repulsed. In a short time, however, he returned to the contest with increased force and determination, but was again foiled and driven back by our skirmishers and Longstreet's reserve companies, which were brought up and employed at the most vigorously assailed points at the critical moment.

It was now that Brigadier General Longstreet sent for reinforcements from Early's Brigade, which I had anticipated by directing the advance of Gen. Early, with two regiments of infantry and two pieces of artillery. As these came upon the field the enemy had advanced a third time with heavy numbers to force Longstreet's position. Hays's Regiment, 7th Louisiana volunteers, which was in advance, was placed on the bank of the stream, under some cover, to the immediate right and left of the ford, relieving Corse's Regiment, 17th Virginia Volunteers; this was done under a heavy fire of musketry, with promising steadiness. The 7th Virginia, under Lieutenant Colonel Williams, was then formed to the right, also under heavy fire, and pushed forward to the stream, relieving the First Regiment Virginia volunteers. At the same time, two rifle guns, brought up with Early's Brigade, were moved down in the field to the right of the road, so as to be concealed from the enemy's artillery by the girth of timber on the immediate bank of the stream, and there opened fire, directed only by the sound of the enemy's musketry. Unable to effect a passage, the enemy kept up a scattering fire for some time. Some of our troops had pushed across the stream, and several small parties of Corse's Regiment, under command of Captain Marye, met and drove the enemy with the bayonet; but as the road-way from the ford was too narrow for a combined movement in force, Gen. Longstreet recalled them to the South bank. Meanwhile, the remainder of Early's infantry and artillery had been called up—that is, six companies of the 24th Regiment Virginia volunteers, under Lieutenant Colonel Hairston, and five pieces of artillery, one rifle gun and four six pounder brass guns, including two six-pounder guns, under Lieutenant Garnett, which had been previously sent to the rear by General Longstreet. This infantry was at once placed in position to the left of the ford, in a space unoccupied by Hays, and the artillery was unlimbered in battery to the right of the road in a line with the two guns already in action. A scattering fire of musketry was still kept up by the enemy for a short time, but that was soon silenced.

It was at this stage of the affair that a remarkable artillery duel was commenced and maintained on our side with a long trained professional opponent, superior in the character as well as in the number of his weapons, provided with improved munitions and every artillery appliance, and at the same time occupying the commanding position. The results were marvellous and fitting precursors to the artillery achievements of the twenty-first of July. In the outset, our fire was directed against the enemy's infantry, whose bayonets, gleaming above the tree tops, alone indicated their presence and force. This drew the attention of a battery placed on a high, commanding ridge, and the duel began in earnest. For a time, the aim of the adversary was inaccurate, but this was quickly corrected and shot fell and shells burst thick and fast in the very midst of our battery, wounding, in the course of the combat, Capt. Eschelman, five privates and the horse of Lieut. Richardson. From the position of our pieces and the nature of the ground, their aim could only be directed at the smoke of the enemy's artillery; how skilfully and with what execution this was done can only be realized by an eye witness. For a few moments, their guns were silenced, but were soon re-opened. By direction of Gen. Longstreet, his battery was then advanced, by hand, out of the range now ascertained by the enemy, and a shower of spherical case shell and round shot flew over the head of our gunners and one of our pieces had become *hors de combat* from an enlarged spent. From this new position our guns fired as before, with no other aim than the smoke and flash of their adversaries' pieces—renewed and urged the conflict with such signal vigor and effect, that gradually the fire of the enemy slackened, the intervals between their discharges grew longer and longer; finally, to cease, and we fired a last gun at a baffled, flying foe, whose heavy masses in the distance were plainly seen to break and scatter in wild confusion and utter rout, strewing the ground with cast-away guns, hats, blankets and knapsacks, as our parting shell was thrown among them. In their retreat, one of their pieces was abandoned, but, from the nature of the ground, it was not sent for that night, and under cover of darkness, the enemy recovered it.

The guns engaged in this singular conflict on our side were three six-pounder rifle pieces and four ordinary six-pounders, all of Walton's Battery—the Washington Artillery of New Orleans. The officers immediately attached, were: Captain Eschelman, Lieutenants C. W. Squires, Richardson, Garnett and Whittington. At the same time, our infantry held the bank of the stream in advance of our guns, and the missiles of the combatants flew to and fro above them, as cool and veteran-like, for more than an hour, they steadily awaited the moment and signal for the advance.

While the conflict was at its height before Blackburn's Ford, about four o'clock, P. M., the enemy again displayed himself in force before Bonham's position. At this, Col. Kershaw, with four companies of his regiment, Second South Carolina, and one piece of Kemper's Battery, were thrown across Mitchell's Ford, to the ridge which Kemper had occupied that morning. Two solid shot and three spherical case, thrown among them—with a precision inaugurated by that artillerist at Vienna—effected their discomfiture and disappearance, and our troops in that quarter were again withdrawn within our lines, having discharged the duty assigned.

At the close of the engagement before Blackburn's Ford, I directed General Longstreet to withdraw the First and Seventeenth Regiments, which had borne the brunt of the action, to a position in reserve, leaving Col. Early to occupy the field with his Brigade and Garland's Regiment.

As a part of the history of this engagement, I desire to place on record, that on the 18th of July not one yard of entrenchment nor one rifle-pit sheltered the men at Blackburn's Ford—who, officers and men, with rare exceptions— were on that day, for the first time, under fire, and who, taking and maintaining every position ordered, cannot be too much commended for their soldierly behavior.

Our artillery was manned and officered by those who, but yesterday, were called from the civil associations of a busy city. They were matched with the picked light artillery of the Federal regular army—Company " E," Third Artillery, under Captain Ayres, with an armament, as their own Chief of Artillery admits, of two ten-pounder Parrott rifle guns, two twelve-pounder Howitzers, and two six-pounder pieces, aided by two twenty-pounder Parrott rifle guns of Company " G," Fifth Artillery, under Lieutenant Benjamin; thus matched, they drove their veteran adversaries from the field, giving confidence in, and promise of the coming efficiency of that brilliant arm of our service.

Having thus related the main or general results and events of the action of Bull Run, in conclusion it is proper to signalize some of those who contributed most to the satisfactory results of that day.

Thanks are due to Brigadier Generals Bonham and Ewell, and Col. Cocke and the officers under them, for the ability shown in conducting and executing the retrogade movements on Bull Run, directed in my orders of the 8th July—movements on which hung the fortunes of this army.

Brigadier General Longstreet, who commanded immediately the troops engaged at Blackburn's Ford on the 18th, equalled my confident expectations, and I may fitly say that by his presence at the right place, at the right moment, among his men, by the exhibition of characteristic coolness, and by his words of encouragement to the men of his command, he infused a confidence and spirit that contributed largely to the success of our arms on that day.

Col. Early brought his brigade into position, and subsequently into action, with judgment; and, at the proper moment, he displayed capacity for command and personal gallantry.

Colonel Moore, commanding the First Virginia Volunteers, was severely wounded at the head of his regiment, the command of which subsequently devolved upon Major Skinner, Lieutenant Colonel Fry having been obliged to leave the field in consequence of a sun stroke.

An accomplished, promising officer, Major Carter H. Harrison, Eleventh Virginia Volunteers, was lost to the service while leading two companies of his regiment against the enemy; he fell, twice shot, mortally wounded.

Brigadier General Longstreet, while finding on all sides alacrity, ardor and intelligence, mentions his special obligations to Colonels Moore, Garland and Corse, commanding, severally, regiments of his brigade, and to the field officers, Lieutenant Colonels Fry, Funsten and Munford, and Majors Brent and Skinner, of whom he says: "They displayed more coolness than is usual among veterans of the old service. General Longstreet also mentions the conduct of Captain Marye, of the Seventeenth Virginia Volunteers, as especialy gallant on one occasion, in advance of the Ford.

The regiments of Early's Brigade were commanded by Colonel Harry Hays and Lieutenant Colonels Williams and Hairston, who handled their commands in action with satisfactory coolness and skill, supported by their field officers, Lieutenant Colonel De Choiseul and Major Penn, of the Seventh Louisiana, and Major Patton of the Seventh Virginia Volunteers.

The skill, the conduct and the soldierly qualities of the Washington Artillery engaged were all that could be desired. The officers and men attached to the seven pieces already specified, won for their battalion a distinction which, I feel assured, will never be tarnished, and which will ever serve to urge them and their corps to high endeavor. Lieutenant Squires worthily commanded the pieces in action.

The commander of the Battalion was necessarily absent from the immediate field, under orders in the sphere of his duties, but the fruits of his discipline, zeal, instruction and capacity as an Artillery Commander was present, and must redound to his reputation.

On the left of Mitchell's Ford, while no serious engagement occurred, the conduct of all was eminently satisfactory to the general officer in command.

It is due, however, to Colonel J. L. Kemper, Virginia forces, to express my sense of the value of his services in the preparation for, and the execution of, the retreat from Fairfax Court House on Bull Run. Called from the head of his regiment, by what appeared to me an imperative need of the service, to take charge of the superior duties of the Quartermaster's Department, with the advance of that critical juncture, he accepted the responsibilities involved, and was eminently efficient.

For further information, touching officers and individuals of the First Brigade, and the details of the retrogade movement, I have to refer particularly to the report of Brigadier General Bonham herewith.

It is proper here to state, that while from the outset it had been determined, on the approach of the enemy in force, to fall back and fight him on the line of Bull Run, yet the position occupied by Gen. Ewell's Brigade, if necessary, could have been maintained against a largely superior force. This was especially the case with the position of the Fifth Alabama Volunteers, Colonel Rhodes, which that excellent officer had made capable of a resolute protracted defence against heavy odds. Accordingly, on the morning of the 17th ultimo, when the enemy appeared before that position, they were checked and held at bay, with some confessed loss, in a skirmish in advance of the works in which Major Morgan and Captain Shelley, Fifth Regiment Alabama Volunteers, acted with intelligent gallantry, and the post was only abandoned under general but specific, imperative orders, in conformity with a long conceived, established plan of action and battle.

Captain E. P. Alexander, Confederate States Engineer, fortunately joined my headquarters in time to introduce the system of new field signals, which, under his skillful management, rendered me the most important service preceding and during the engagement.

The medical officers serving with the regiments engaged were at their proper posts, and discharged their duties with satisfactory skill and zeal, and, on one occasion at least, under an annoying fire; when Surgeon Cullen, First Regiment Virginia Volunteers, was obliged to remove our wounded from the hospital, which had become the special target of the enemy's rifle guns, notwithstanding it was surmounted by the usual yellow flag, but which, however, I hope, for the sake of past relations was ignorantly mistaken for the Confederate flag. The name of each individual medical officer I cannot mention.

On the day of the engagement, I was attended by my personal staff, Lieutenant S. W. Ferguson, A. D. C., and my volunteer Aids de Camp, Colonels Preston, Chesnut, Manning, Miles, Chisholm and Heyward, of South Carolina, to all of whom I am greatly indebted for manifold essential services in the transmission of orders on the field, and in the preliminary arrangements for the occupation and maintenance of the line of Bull Run.

Colonel Thomas Jordan, Assistant Adjutant General; Captain C. N. Smith, Assistant Adjutant General; Colonel S. Jones, Chief of Artillery and Ordnance; Major Cabell, Chief Quartermaster; Captain W. H. Fowle, Chief of Subsistence Department; Surgeon Thomas H. Williams, Medical Director, and Assistant Surgeon Brodie, Medical Purveyor of the General Staff, attached to the Army of the Potomac, were necessarily engaged, severally, with their responsible duties at my headquarters at Camp Pickens, which they discharged with an energy and intelligence for which I have to tender my sincere thanks.

Messrs. McLean, Wilcoxen, Kinchcloe and Brawner, citizens of this immediate vicinity, it is their due to say, have placed me and the country under great obligation for the information relative to this region, which has enabled me to avail myself of its defensive features and resources. They were found ever ready to give me their time, without stint or reward.

Our casualties, in all, sixty-eight killed and wounded, were fifteen* killed and fifty-three wounded, several of whom have since died. The loss of the enemy can only be conjectured; it was unquestionably heavy. In the cursory examination which was made by details from Longstreet's and Early's Brigades, on the 18th July, of that of the field immediately contested and near Blackburn's Ford, some sixty-four corpses were found and buried, and at least twenty prisoners were also picked up, besides, 175 stands of arms, a large quantity of accoutrements and blankets, and quite one hundred and fifty hats.

The effect of this day's conflict was to satisfy the enemy that he could not force a passage across Bull Run in the face of our troops, and led him into the flank movement of the 21st July and the battle of Manassas, the details of which will be related in another paper.

Herewith I have the honor to transmit the reports of the several Brigade Commanders engaged, and of Artillery. Also, a map of the field of battle.

The rendition of this report, it is proper to say in conclusion, has been unavoidably delayed by the constantly engrossing administrative duties of the commander of an army corps composed wholly of volunteers—duties vitally essential to its well being and future efficiency, and which I could not set aside or postpone on any account.

I have the honor to be, Gen., your ob'dt. serv't,
G. T. BEAUREGARD,
Gen'l S. COOPER, Adj't and Insp'r Gen'l, C. S. A.

---

*Including two reported "missing,"

OFFICIAL REPORT OF THE BATTLE OF MANASSAS, JULY 21st, 1861—J. E. JOHNSTON, GENERAL COMMANDING.

HEADQUARTERS ARMY OF THE POTOMAC,
FAIRFAX C. H., October 14th, 1861.

To the Adjutant and Inspector General
Confederate States Army :

SIR: I have the honor to submit to the honorable Secretary of War a report of the operations of the troops under my command which terminated in the battle of Manassas.

I assumed command at Harper's Ferry on the 23d of May. The force at that point then, consisted of nine regiments and two battalions of infantry, four companies of artillery with sixteen pieces, without caissons, harness or horses, and about three hundred cavalry. They were of course undisciplined; several regiments without accoutrements, and with an entirely inadequate supply of ammunition.

I lost no time in making a complete reconnoisance of the place and its environs, in which the Chief Engineer, Major (now Brigadier General) Whiting ably assisted. The results confirmed my preconceived ideas.

The position is untenable by any force not strong

enough to take the field against an invading army and to hold both sides of the Potomac. It is a triangle, two sides being formed by the Potomac and the Shenandoah, and the third by Furnace Ridge. The plateau thus enclosed, and the end of Furnace Ridge itself, the only defensible position, which, however, required for its adequate occupation double our numbers, was exposed to enfilade and reverse fires of artillery from heights on the Maryland side of the river. Within that line, the ground was more favorable to an attacking than to a defending force. The Potomac can be easily crossed at many points above and below, so that it is easily turned. It is twenty miles from the great route into the Valley of Virginia from Pennsylvania and Maryland, by which General Patterson's approach was expected. Its garrison was thus out of position to defend that valley, or to prevent General McClellan's junction with General Patterson. These were the obvious and important objects to be kept in view. Besides being in position for them, it was necessary to be able, on emergency, to join General Beauregard.

The occupation of Harper's Ferry by our army perfectly suited the enemy's views. We were bound to a fixed point. His movements were unrestricted. These views were submitted to the military authorities. The continued occupation of the place was, however, deemed by them indispensable. I determined to hold it until the great objects of the Government required its abandonment.

The practicable roads from the West and Northwest, as well as from Manassas, meet the route from Pennsylvania and Maryland at Winchester. That point was, therefore, in my opinion, our best position.

The distinguished commander of the army of the Potomac was convinced, like myself, of our dependence upon each other, and promised to co-operate with me in case of need. To guard against surprise, and to impose upon the enemy, Major Whiting was directed to mount a few heavy guns upon Furnace Ridge, and otherwise strengthen the position.

I was employed, until the 13th of June, in continuing what had been begun by my predecessor, Col. (now Major General) Jackson, the organization, instruction and equipment of the troops, and providing means of transportation and artillery horses. The river was observed from the Point of Rocks to the Western part of the county of Berkeley—the most distant portions by the indefatigable Stuart with his cavalry. General Patterson's troops were within a few hours of Williamsport, and General McClellan's in Western Virginia were supposed to be approaching to effect a junction with Patterson, whose force was reported, by well informed persons, to be eighteen thousand men.

On the morning of the 13th of June, information was received from Winchester, that Romney was occupied by two thousand Federal troops, supposed to be the van-guard of McClellan's army.

Colonel A. P. Hill, with his own (13th) and Colonel Gibbon's (10th) Virginia Regiments, was despatched by railway to Winchester. He was directed to move thence towards Romney, to take the best position and best measures to check the advance of the enemy. He was to add to his command the 3d Tennessee Regiment, which had just arrived at Winchester.

During that day and the next, the heavy baggage and remaining public property were sent to Winchester by the railway, and the bridges on the Potomac destroyed. On the morning of the 15th, the army left Harper's Ferry for Winchester, (the force had been increased by three regiments since the 1st of June) and bivouacked four miles beyond Charlestown. On the morning of the 16th, intelligence was received that General Patterson's army had crossed the Potomac at Williamsport, also that the United States force at Romney had fallen back. A courier from Richmond brought a despatch authorizing me to evacuate Harper's Ferry at my discretion.

The army was ordered to gain the Martinsburg Turnpike, by a flank movement to Bunker's Hill, in order to place itself between Winchester and the expected advance of Patterson. On hearing of this, the enemy re-crossed the river precipitately. Resuming my first direction and plan, I proceeded to Winchester. There the army was in position to oppose either McClellan from the West, or Patterson from the Northeast, and to form a junction with General Beauregard when necessary.

Lieutenant Colonel George Stewart, with his Maryland Battalion, was sent to Harper's Ferry to bring off some public property said to have been left. As McClellan was moving Southwestward from Grafton, Colonel Hill's command was withdrawn from Romney. The defence of that region of country was entrusted to Colonel McDonald's Regiment of Cavalry. Intelligence from Maryland indicating another movement by Patterson, Colonel Jackson, with his brigade, was sent to the neighborhood of Martinsburg, to support Col. Stuart. The latter officer had been placed in observation on the line of the Potomac with his cavalry. His increasing vigilance and activity was relied on to repress small incursions of the enemy, to give intelligence of invasion by them, and to watch, harrass and circumscribe their every movement. Colonel Jackson was instructed to destroy such of the rolling stock of the Baltimore and Ohio Railroad as could not be brought off, and to have so much of it as could be made available to our service brought to Winchester.

Major Whiting was ordered to plan defensive works and to have some heavy guns on navy carriages mounted. About twenty-five hundred militia, under Brigadier General Carson, were called out from Frederick and the neighboring counties to man them.

On the 2d of July, General Patterson again crossed the Potomac. Colonel Jackson, pursuant to instructions, fell back before him. In retiring, he gave him a severe lesson, in the affair at Falling Waters. With a battalion of the 5th Virginia Regiment (Harper's), and Pendleton's Battery of Field Artillery, he engaged the enemy's advance. Skillfully taking a position where the smallness of his force was concealed, he engaged them for a considerable time, inflicted a heavy loss, and retired when about to be outflanked, scarcely losing a man, but bringing off forty-five prisoners.

Upon this intelligence the army, strengthened by the arrival of General Bee and Colonel Elzey, and the 9th Georgia Regiment, was ordered forward to the support of Jackson. It met him at Darksville, six miles from Martinsburg, where it took up a position for action, as General Patterson, it was supposed, was closely following Colonel Jackson. We waited for him in this position four days, hoping to be attacked by an adversary at least double our number, but unwilling to attack him in a town so defensible as Martinsburg, with its solid buildings and enclosures of masonry. Convinced at length that he would not approach us, I returned to Winchester, much to the disappointment of our troops, who were eager for battle with the invaders. Colonel Stuart, with his cavalry, as usual, remained near the enemy.

Before the 15th of July, the enemy's force, according to the best intelligence to be obtained, amounted to about thirty-two thousand. Ours had been increased by eight Southern regiments. On the 15th of July, Colonel Stuart reported the advance of General Patterson from Martinsburg. He halted, however, at Bunker's Hill, nine miles from Winchester, where he remained on the 16th. On the 17th, he moved his left to Smithfield. This created the impression that he intended to attack us on the south, or was merely holding us in check, while General Beauregard should be attacked at Manassas by General Scott.

About one o'clock on the morning of July 18th, I received from the Government a telegraphic dispatch, informing me that the Northern army was advancing upon Manassas, then held by General Beauregard, and directing me, if practicable, to go to that officer's assistance, sending my sick to Culpeper Courthouse.

In the exercise of the discretion conferred by the terms of the order, I at once determined to march to join General Beauregard. The best service which the army of the Shenandoah could render, was to prevent the defeat of that of the Potomac. To be able to do this, it was necessary, in the first instance, to defeat General Patterson, or to elude him. The latter course was the most speedy and certain, and was therefore adopted. Our sick, nearly seventeen hundred in number, were provided for in Winchester. For the defence of that place, the militia of Generals Carson and Meem seemed ample; for I thought it certain that General Patterson would follow my movement, as soon as he discovered it. Evading him, by the disposition made of the advance guard under Colonel Stuart, the army moved through Ashby's Gap to Piedmont, a station of the Manassas Gap Railroad. Hence, the infantry were to be transported by the railway, while the cavalry and artillery were ordered to continue their march. I reached Manassas about noon on the 20th, preceded by the 7th and 8th Georgia regiments, and by Jackson's brigade, consisting of the 2nd, 4th, 5th, 27th and 33rd Virginia regiments. I was accompanied by General Bee, with the 4th Alabama, the 2nd and two companies of the 11th Mississippi. The president of the railroad company had assured me that the remaining troops should arrive during the day.

I found General Beauregard's position too extensive, and the ground too densely wooded and intricate, to be learned in the brief time at my disposal, and therefore determined to rely upon his knowledge of it, and of the enemy's positions. This I did readily, from full confidence in his capacity.

His troops were divided into eight brigades, occupying the defensive line of Bull Run. Brigadier-General Ewell's was posted at the Union Mills Ford; Brigadier-General D. R. Jones's at McLean's Ford; Brigadier-General Longstreet's at Blackburn's Ford; Brigadier-General Bonham's at Mitchell's Ford; Colonel Cocke's at Ball's Ford, some three miles above, and Colonel Evans, with a regiment and battalion, formed the extreme left at the Stone Bridge. The brigades of Brigadier-General Holmes, and

Colonel Early, were in reserve, in rear of the right. I regarded the arrival of the remainder of the army of the Shenandoah, during the night, as certain, and Patterson's junction with the Grand Army, on the 22nd, as probable. During the evening it was determined, instead of remaining in the defensive positions then occupied, to assume the offensive, and attack the enemy before such a junction.

General Beauregard proposed a plan of battle, which I approved without hesitation. He drew up the necessary order during the night, which was approved formally by me at half-past four o'clock on the morning of the 21st. The early movements of the enemy on that morning, and the non-arrival of the expected troops, prevented its execution. General Beauregard afterwards proposed a modification of the abandoned plan—to attack with our right, while the left stood on the defensive. This, too, became impracticable, and a battle ensued, different in place and circumstance from any previous plan on our side.

Soon after sunrise, on the morning of the 21st, a light cannonade was opened upon Colonel Evans's position; a similar demonstration was made against the centre soon after, and strong forces were observed in front of it and of the right. About eight o'clock, General Beauregard and I placed ourselves on a commanding hill in rear of General Bonham's left. Near nine o'clock the signal officer, Captain Alexander, reported that a large body of troops was crossing the valley of Bull Run, some two miles above the bridge. General Bee, who had been placed near Colonel Cocke's position, Colonel Hampton, with his legion, and Colonel Jackson, from a point near Gen. Bonham's left, were ordered to hasten to the left flank.

The signal officer soon called our attention to a heavy cloud of dust to the north-west, and about ten miles off, such as the march of an army would raise. This excited apprehensions of General Patterson's approach.

The enemy, under cover of a strong demonstration on our right, made a long detour through the woods on his right, crossed Bull Run two miles above our left, and threw himself upon the flank and rear of our position. This movement was fortunately discovered in time for us to check its progress, and ultimately to form a new line of battle nearly at right angles with the defensive line of Bull Run.

On discovering that the enemy had crossed the stream above him, Colonel Evans moved to his left with eleven companies and two field pieces, to oppose his advance, and disposed his little force under cover of the wood, near the intersection of the Warrenton Turnpike and the Sudley Road. Here he was attacked by the enemy in immensely superior numbers, against which he maintained himself with skill and unshrinking courage. General Bee, moving towards the enemy, guided by the firing, had, with a soldier's eye, selected the position near the Henry House, and formed his troops upon it. They were the 7th and 8th Georgia, 4th Alabama, 2nd Mississippi, and two companies of the 11th Mississippi Regiments, with Imboden's battery. Being compelled, however, to sustain Colonel Evans, he crossed the valley and formed on the right and somewhat in advance of his position. Here the joint force, little exceeding five regiments, with six field pieces, held the ground against about fifteen thousand United States troops for an hour, until, finding themselves outflanked by the continually arriving troops of the enemy, they fell back to General Bee's first position, upon the line of which, Jackson, just arriving, formed his brigade and Stanard's battery. Colonel Hampton, who had by this time advanced with his Legion as far as the Turnpike, rendered efficient service in maintaining the orderly character of the retreat from that point; and here fell the gallant Lieutenant Colonel Johnson, his second in command.

In the meantime, I awaited with General Beauregard, near the centre, the full development of the enemy's designs. About 11 o'clock, the violence of the firing on the left indicated a battle, and the march of a large body of troops from the enemy's centre towards the conflict, was shown by clouds of dust. I was thus convinced, that his great effort was to be made with his right. I stated that conviction to General Beauregard, and the absolute necessity of immediately strengthening our left as much as possible. Orders were, accordingly, at once sent General Holmes and Colonel Early, to move with all speed to the sound of the firing, and to General Bonham to send up two of his regiments and a battery. Gen. Beauregard and I then hurried at a rapid gallop to the scene of action, about four miles off. On the way, I directed my chief of artillery, Colonel Pendleton, to follow with his own and Alburtis's batteries. We came not a moment too soon: The long contest, against five-fold odds and heavy losses, especially of field officers, had greatly discouraged the troops of General Bee and Colonel Evans. Our presence with them under fire, and some example, had the happiest effect on the spirit of the troops. Order was soon restored, and the battle re-established, to which the firmness of Jackson's brigade greatly contributed. Then, in a brief and rapid conference, General Beauregard was assigned to the command of the left, which, as the younger officer, he claimed, while I returned to that of the whole field. The aspect of affairs was critical, but I had full confidence in the skill and indomitable courage of General Beauregard, the high soldierly qualities of Generals Bee and Jackson, and Colonel Evans, and the devoted patriotism of their troops. Orders were first dispatched to hasten the march of General Holmes's, Colonel Early's and General Bonham's Regiments. General Ewell was also directed to follow with all speed. Many of the broken troops, fragments of companies, and individual stragglers, were reformed and brought into action, with the aid of my staff, and a portion of General Beauregard's. Colonel (Governor) Smith, with his battalion, and Colonel Hunton, with his regiment, were ordered up to reinforce the right. I have since learned that General Beauregard had previously ordered them into the battle. They belonged to his corps. Colonel Smith's cheerful courage had a fine influence, not only upon the spirit of his own men, but upon the stragglers from the troops engaged. The largest body of these, equal to about four companies, having no competent field officer, I placed under command of one of my staff, Colonel F. J. Thomas, who fell, while gallantly leading it against the enemy. These reinforcements were all sent to the right, to re-establish, more perfectly, that part of our line. Having attended to these pressing duties, at the immediate scene of conflict, my eye was next directed to Colonel Cocke's brigade, the nearest at hand. Hastening to his position, I desired him to lead his troops into action. He informed me, however, that a large body of the enemy's troops, beyond the stream and below the bridge, threatened us from that quarter. He was, therefore, left in his position.

My headquarters were now established near the Lewis House. From this commanding elevation, my view embraced the position of the enemy beyond the stream, and the approaches to the Stone Bridge, a point of especial importance. I could also see the advances of our troops, far down the valley, in the direction of Manassas, and observe the progress of the action and the manœuvres of the enemy.

We had now sixteen guns, and two hundred and sixty cavalry, and a little above nine regiments of the army of the Shenandoah, and six guns, and less than the strength of three regiments, of that of the Potomac, engaged with about thirty-five thousand United States troops, amongst whom, were full three thousand men of the old regular army. Yet, this admirable artillery, and brave infantry and cavalry, lost no foot of ground. For nearly three hours they maintained their position, repelling five successive assaults, by the heavy masses of the enemy, whose numbers enabled him continually to bring up fresh troops, as their preceding columns were driven back. Colonel Stuart contributed to one of these repulses, by a well timed and vigorous charge on the enemy's right flank, with two companies of his cavalry. The efficiency of our infantry and cavalry, might have been expected from a patriotic people, accustomed, like ours, to the management of arms and horses, but that of the artillery, was little less than wonderful. They were opposed to batteries far superior, in the number, range and equipment of their guns, with educated officers, and thoroughly instructed soldiers. We had but one educated artillerist, Colonel Pendleton—that model of a Christian soldier—yet they exhibited as much superiority to the enemy in skill as in courage. Their fire was superior, both in rapidity and precision.

About two o'clock, an officer of General Beauregard's Adjutant General's office, galloped from Manassas, to report to me that a United States army had reached the line of the Manassas Gap Railroad, was marching towards us, and then but three or four miles from our left flank.

The expected reinforcements appeared soon after. Col. Cocke was then desired to lead his brigade into action, to support the right of the troops engaged, which he did, with alacrity and effect. Within a half hour, the two regiments of General Bonham's brigade, (Cash's and Kershaw's,) came up, and were directed against the enemy's right, which he seemed to be strengthening. Fisher's North Carolina regiment was, soon after, sent in the same direction. About three o'clock, while the enemy seemed to be striving to outflank and drive back our left, and thus separate us from Manassas, General E. K. Smith arrived, with three regiments of Elzey's brigade. He was instructed to attack the right flank of the enemy, now exposed to us. Before the movement was completed, he fell, severely wounded. Colonel Elzey at once taking command, executed it with great promptitude and vigor. General Beauregard rapidly seized the opportunity thus afforded him, and threw forward his whole line. The enemy was driven back from the long contested hill, and victory was no longer doubtful. He made yet another attempt to retrieve the day. He again extended his right, with a still wider sweep, to turn our left. Just as he re-formed, to renew the battle, Colonel Early's three regiments came upon the field. The enemy's new formation exposed his right flank more even than the previous one. Colonel Early was, therefore, ordered to throw himself directly upon it, supported by Colonel Stuart's cavalry, and Beckham's battery. He executed this attack bravely and well, while a simultaneous charge was made by General Beauregard in front. The enemy was broken by this combined attack. He lost all the artillery which he had advanced to the scene of the conflict. He had no more fresh troops to rally on, and a general rout ensued.

Instructions were instantly sent to General Bonham, to march by the quickest route to the turnpike, to intercept the fugitives; and to General Longstreet, to follow as closely as possible upon the right. Their progress was checked by the enemy's reserve, and by night, at Centreville.

Schenck's brigade made a slight demonstration towards Lewis's ford, which was quickly checked by Holmes's brigade, which had just arrived from the right. His artillery, under Captain Walker, was used with great skill.

Colonel Stuart pressed the pursuit on the enemy's principal line of retreat, the Sudley Road. Four companies of cavalry, under Colonel Radford and Lieutenant-Colonel Munford, which I had held in reserve, were ordered to cross the stream at Ball's Ford, to reach the turnpike, the line of retreat of the enemy's left. Our cavalry found the roads encumbered with dead and wounded, (many of whom seemed to have been thrown from wagons,) arms, accoutrements and clothing.

A report came to me from the right, that a strong body of United States troops was advancing upon Manassas. General Holmes, who had just reached the field, and General Ewell on his way to it, were ordered to meet this unexpected attack. They found no foe, however.

Our victory was as complete as one gained by infantry and artillery can be. An adequate force of cavalry would have made it decisive.

It is due, under Almighty God, to the skill and resolution of General Beauregard, the admirable conduct of Generals Bee, E. K. Smith and Jackson, and of Colonels (commanding brigades) Evans, Cocke, Early and Elzey, and the courage and unyielding firmness of our patriotic volunteers. The admirable character of our troops is incontestibly proved by the result of this battle; especially when it is remembered that little more than six thousand men of the army of the Shenandoah, with sixteen guns, and less than two thousand of that of the Potomac, with six guns, for full five hours successfully resisted thirty-five thousand United States troops, with a powerful artillery, and a superior force of regular cavalry. Our forces engaged, gradually increasing during the remainder of the contest, amounted to but ———— men at the close of the battle. The brunt of this hard-fought engagement fell upon the troops who held their ground so long, with such heroic resolution. The unfading honor which they won, was dearly bought with the blood of many of our best and bravest. Their loss was far heavier, in proportion, than that of the troops coming later into action.

Every regiment and battery engaged performed its part well. The commanders of brigades have been already mentioned. I refer you to General Beauregard's report, for the names of the officers of the army of the Potomac, who distinguished themselves most. I cannot enumerate all of the army of the Shenandoah, who deserve distinction, and will confine myself to those of high rank. Colonels Bartow and Fisher, (killed,) Jones, (mortally wounded,) Harper, J. F. Preston, Cummings, Falkner, Gartrell and Vaughan; J. E. B. Stuart, of the cavalry, and Pendleton of the artillery, Lieutenant-Colonel Echols, Lightfoot, Lackland, G. H. Stewart and Gardner. The last-named gallant officer was severely wounded.

The loss of the army of the Potomac was, 108 killed, 510 wounded, 12 missing. That of the army of the Shenandoah was, 270 killed, 979 wounded, 18 missing.

Total killed,	378
" wounded,	1,489
" missing,	30

That of the enemy could not be ascertained. It must have been between four and five thousand. Twenty-eight pieces of artillery, about five thousand muskets, and nearly five hundred thousand cartridges; a garrison flag and ten colors were captured on the field or in the pursuit. Besides these, we captured sixty-four artillery horses, with their harness, twenty-six wagons, and much camp equipage, clothing, and other property, abandoned in their flight.

The officers of my staff deserve high commendation for their efficient and gallant services during the day and the campaign, and I beg leave to call the attention of the Government to their merits. Major W. H. C. Whiting, Chief Engineer, was invaluable to me, for his signal ability in his profession, and for his indefatigable activity before and in the battle. Major McClean, Chief Quartermaster, and Major

Kearsley, Chief Commissary, conducted their respective departments with skill and energy. Major Rhett, A. A. General, who joined me only the day before, was of great service. I left him at Manassas, and to his experience and energy I entrusted the care of ordering my troops to the field of battle as they should arrive, and forwarding ammunition for the artillery during the action. Captains C. M. Fauntleroy, C. S. Navy, T. L. Preston, A. A. A. General, and Lieutenant J. B. Washington, A. D. C., conveyed my orders bravely and well, on this their first field, as did several gallant gentlemen who volunteered their services—Colonel Cole of Florida, Major Deas of Alabama, Colonel Duncan, of Kentucky. Lieutenant Beverly Randolph, C. S. N., aided Colonel F. J. Thomas in the command of the body of troops he led into action, and fought with gallantry. With these was my gallant friend, Captain Barlow Mason, who was mortally wounded. I have already mentioned the brave death of ordnance officer Colonel F. J. Thomas. I was much indebted, also, to Colonels J. J. Preston, Manning, Miles and Chisholm, and Captain Stevens, of the Engineer Corps, members of General Beauregard's staff, who kindly proffered their services, and rendered efficient and valuable aid, at different times during the day. Colonel G. W. Lay, of General Bonham's staff, delivered my instructions to the troops sent in pursuit and to intercept the enemy, with much intelligence and courage.

It will be remarked that the three Brigadier-Generals of the army of the Shenandoah were all wounded. I have already mentioned the wound of General Smith. General Jackson, though painfully wounded early in the day, commanded his brigade to the close of the action. General Bee, after great exposure at the commencement of the engagement, was mortally wounded, just as our reinforcements were coming up.

The apparent firmness of the United States troops at Centreville, who had not been engaged, which checked our pursuit; the strong forces occupying the works near Georgetown, Arlington and Alexandria; the certainty, too, that General Patterson, if needed, would reach Washington, with his army of thirty thousand men, sooner than we could; and the condition and inadequate means of the army in ammunition, provisions and transportation, prevented any serious thoughts of advancing against the Capital. It is certain that the fresh troops within the works were, in number, quite sufficient for their defence; if not, General Patterson's army would certainly reinforce them soon enough.

This report will be presented to you by my Aid-de-Camp, Lieutenant J. B. Washington, by whom, and by General Beauregard's Aid, Lieutenant Ferguson, the captured colors are transmitted to the War Department.

Most respectfully,
Your ob't serv't,
(Signed,) J. E. JOHNSTON,
General.

(Official.) R. H. CHILTON,
A. A. General.

REPORT OF GEN. BEAUREGARD, OF THE BATTLE OF MANASSAS.

———•••———

Headquarters 1st Corps Army of the Potomac,
Manassas, August 26th, 1861.

General:

* * * * * * * *

* * * * * * * *

The War Department having been informed by me, by telegraph on the 17th of July, of the movement of Gen. McDowell—Gen. Johnston was immediately ordered to form a junction of his Army Corps with mine, should the movement, in his judgment, be deemed advisable. Gen. Holmes was also directed to push forward with two regiments, a battery, and one company of cavalry.

In view of these propositions, approaching reinforcements, modifying my plan of operations, so far as to determine on attacking the enemy at Centreville, as soon as I should hear of the near approach of the two reinforcing columns, I sent one of my Aids, Col. Chisholm, of South Carolina, to meet and communicate my plans to Gen. Johnston, and my wish that one portion of his forces should march by the way of Aldie, and take the enemy on his right flank and in reverse at Centreville. Difficulties, however, of an insuperable character, in connection with means of transportation, and the marching condition of his troops, made this impracticable, and it was determined our forces should be united within the lines of Bull Run, and thence advance to the attack of the enemy.

Gen. Johnston arrived here about noon on the 20th July, and being my senior in rank, he necessarily assumed command of all the forces of the Confederate States, then concentrating at this point. Made acquainted with my plan of operations and dispositions to meet the enemy, he gave them his entire approval, and generously directed their execution under my command.

In consequence of the untoward detention, however, of some (5,000) five thousand of General Johnston's Army Corps, resulting from the inadequate and imperfect means of transportation for so many troops, at the disposition of the Manassas Gap Railroad, it became necessary, on the morning of the 21st, before daylight, to modify the plan accepted, to suit the contingency of an immediate attack on our lines, by the main force of the enemy, then plainly at hand.

The enemy's forces, reported by their best informed journals to be 55,000 strong, I had learned from reliable sources, on the night of the 20th, were being concentrated in and around Centreville, and along the Warrenton Turnpike road, to Bull Run, near which, our respective pickets were in immediate proximity. This fact, with the conviction that, after his signal discomfiture on the 18th of July, before Blackburn's Ford—the centre of my lines—he would not renew the attack in that quarter, induced me at once to look for an attempt on my left flank, resting on the Stone Bridge, which was but weakly guarded by men, as well as but slightly provided with artificial defensive appliances and artillery.

In view of these palpable military conditions, by half-past four, A. M., on the 21st July, I had prepared and dispatched orders, directing the whole of the Confederate forces within the lines of Bull Run, including the brigades and regiments of Gen. Johnston, which had arrived at that time, to be held in readiness to march at a moment's notice.

At that hour, the following was the disposition of our forces:

Ewell's Brigade, constituted as on the 18th July, remained in position at Union Mills Ford, its left extending along Bull Run in the direction of McLean's Ford, and supported by Holmes's Brigade, 2nd Tennessee and 1st Arkansas Regiments, a short distance to the rear—that is, at and near Camp Wigfall.

D. R. Jones's Brigade—from Ewell's left, in front of McLean's Ford, and along the stream to Longstreet's position. It was unchanged in organization, and was supported by Early's Brigade—also unchanged—placed behind a thicket of young pines, a short distance in the rear of McLean's Ford.

Longstreet's Brigade held its former ground at Blackburn's Ford, from Jones's left to Bonham's right, at Mitchell's Ford, and was supported by Jackson's Brigade, consist-ing of Colonels James L. Preston's 4th, Harper's 5th, Allen's 2nd, the 27th, (Lieut. Col. Echol's,) and the 33rd, (Cumming's,) Virginia Regiments, 2,611 strong, which were posted behind the skirting of pines, to the rear of Blackburn's and Mitchell's Ford; and in rear of this support was, also, Barksdale's 13th Regiment Mississippi Volunteers, which had lately arrived from Lynchburg.

Along the edge of a pine thicket, in rear of, and equi-distant from McLean's and Blackburn's Fords, ready to support either position, I had also placed all of Bee's and Bartow's Brigades that had arrived, namely: two companies of the 11th Mississippi, Lieut. Col. Liddell; the 2nd Mississippi, Col. Falkner, and the 4th Alabama, with the 7th and 8th Georgia Regiments, (Colonels Gartrell and Lieut. Col. Gardner,) in all 2,732 bayonets.

Bonham's Brigade, as before, held Mitchell's Ford, its right near Longstreet's left, its left extending in the direction of Cocke's right. It was organized as at the end of the 18th of July, with Jackson's Brigade, as before said, as a support.

Cocke's Brigade, increased by seven companies of the 8th, (Hunton's,) three companies of the 49th, (Smith's,) Virginia Regiments, two companies of cavalry, and a battery under Rogers, of four 6-pounders, occupied the line in front and rear of Bull Run, extending from the direction of Bonham's left, and guarding Island, Ball's and Lewis's Fords, to the right of Evans's Demi-Brigade near the Stone Bridge, also under General Cocke's command.

The latter held the Stone Bridge, and its left covered a farm ford about one mile above the bridge.

Stuart's cavalry, some three hundred men of the Army of the Shenandoah, guarded the level ground extending in rear from Bonham's left to Cocke's right.

Two companies of Radford's cavalry were held in reserve, a short distance in rear of Mitchell's Ford, his left extending in the direction of Stuart's right.

Colonel Pendleton's reserve battery, of eight pieces, was temporarily placed in rear of Bonham's extreme left.

Major Walton's reserve battery, of five guns, was in position on McLean's farm, in a piece of woods in rear of Bee's right.

Hampton's Legion, of six companies of infantry, six hundred strong, having arrived that morning, by the cars, from Richmond, was subsequently, as soon as it arrived, ordered forward to a position in immediate vicinity of the Lewis House, as a support for any troops engaged in that quarter.

The effective force of all arms, of the Army of the Potomac, on that eventful morning, including the garrison of Camp Pickens, did not exceed 21,833, and 29 guns.

The Army of the Shenandoah, ready for action on the field, may be set at 6,000 men, and 20 guns.*

The Brigade of General Holmes mustered about 1,265 bayonets, six guns, and a company of cavalry, about 90 strong.

Informed at 5.30, A. M., by Colonel Evans, that the enemy had deployed some twelve hundred men,† with several pieces of artillery, in his immediate front, I at once ordered him, as also General Cocke, if attacked, to maintain their position to the last extremity.

---

* That is, when the battle began—Smith's Brigade and Fisher's North Carolina, came up later, and made total of army of Shenandoah engaged, of all arms, 8,334. Hill's Virginia Regiment, 550, also arrived, but was posted as reserve to right flank.

† These were what Colonel Evans saw of General Schenck's Brigade of General Tyler's Division, and two other heavy brigades, in all, over 9,000 men, and 13 pieces of artillery—Carlisle's and Ayres's Batteries. That is, 900 men, and two 6-pounders, confronted by 9,000 men, and thirteen pieces of artillery, mostly rifled.

In my opinion, the most effective method of relieving that flank was by a rapid, determined attack with my right wing and centre on the enemy's flank and rear at Centreville, with due precautions against the advance of his reserves from the direction of Washington. By such a movement, I confidently expected to achieve a complete victory for my country by 12, M.

These new dispositions were submitted to General Johnston, who fully approved them, and the orders for their immediate execution were at once issued.

Brigadier General Ewell was directed to begin the movement, to be followed and supported successively by Generals D. R. Jones, Longstreet and Bonham, respectively, supported by their several appointed reserves.

The cavalry under Stuart and Radford were to be held in hand, subject to future orders and ready for employment, as might be required by the exigencies of the battle.

About 8.30, A. M., General Johnston and myself transferred our headquarters to a central position about half a mile in rear of Mitchell's Ford, whence we might watch the course of events.

Previously, as early as 5.30, the Federalists in front of Evans's position—Stone Bridge—had opened with a large 30-pounder Parrot rifle gun, and thirty minutes later, with a moderate, apparently tentative fire, from a battery of rifle pieces, directed first in front at Evans's, and then in the direction of Cocke's position, but without drawing a return fire and discovery of our positions, chiefly because in that quarter we had nothing but eight 6-pounder pieces, which could not reach the distant enemy.

As the Federalists had advanced with an extended line of skirmishers in front of Evans, that officer promptly threw forward the two flank companies of the 4th South Carolina Regiment and one company of Wheat's Louisiana Battalion, deployed as skirmishers, to cover his small front. An occasional scattering fire resulted, and thus stood the two armies in that quarter for more than an hour, while the main body of the enemy was marching his devious way through the "Big Forest" to take our forces in flank and rear.

By 8.30, A. M., Colonel Evans, having become satisfied of the counterfeit character of the movement on his front, and persuaded of an attempt to turn his left flank, decided to change his position to meet the enemy, and for this purpose immediately put in motion to his left and rear six companies of Sloan's 4th South Carolina Regiment, Wheat's Louisiana Battalion, five companies, and two 6-pounders of Latham's Battery, leaving four companies of Sloan's Regiment under cover as the sole, immediate defence of the Stone Bridge, but giving information to General Cocke of his change of position, and the reasons that impelled it.

Following a road leading by the Old Pittsylvania (Carter) Mansion, Colonel Evans formed in line of battle some four hundred yards in rear—as he advanced—of that house, his guns to the front and in position, properly supported, to its immediate right. Finding, however, that the enemy did not appear on that road, which was a branch of one leading by Sudley's Springs Ford to Brentsville and Dumfries, he turned abruptly to the left, and, marching across the fields for three-quarters of a mile—about 9.30, A. M.—took a position in line of battle; his left, Sloan's companies, resting on the main Brentsville Road in a shallow ravine, the Louisiana Battalion to the right, in advance some two hundred yards, a rectangular copse of wood separating them. One piece of his artillery, planted on an eminence some seven hundred yards to the rear of Wheat's Battalion, and the other on a ridge near, and in rear of Sloan's position, commanding a reach of the road just in front of the line of battle. In this order he awaited the coming of the masses of the enemy, now drawing near.

In the meantime, about 7 o'clock, A. M., Jackson's Brigade, with Imboden's, and five pieces of Walton's Battery, had been sent to take up a position along Bull Run to guard the interval between Cocke's right and Bonham's left, with orders to support either, in case of need—the character and topographical features of the ground having been shown to General Jackson, by Captain D. B. Harris, of the Engineers of this Army Corps.

So much of Bee's and Bartow's Brigades, now united, as had arrived—some 2,800 muskets—had also been sent forward to the support of the position of the Stone Bridge.

The enemy, beginning his detour from the turnpike, at a point nearly half-way between Stone Bridge and Centreville, had pursued a tortuous, narrow trace of a rarely used road, through a dense wood, the greater part of his way until near the Sudley Road. A division, under Colonel Hunter, of the Federal Regular Army, of two strong brigades, was in the advance, followed immediately by another division, under Colonel Heintzelman, of three brigades, and seven companies of regular cavalry, and twenty-four pieces of artillery—eighteen of which were rifle guns.

This column, as it crossed Bull Run, numbered over 16,000 men, of all arms, by their own accounts.

Burnside's Brigade—which here, as at Fairfax C. H., led the advance—at about 9.45, A. M., debouched from a wood in sight of Evans's position, some 500 yards distant from Wheat's Battalion.

He immediately threw forward his skirmishers in force, and they became engaged with Wheat's command, and the 6-pounder gun, under Lieutenant Leftwitch.

The Federalists at once advanced, as they report officially, the 2d Rhode Island Regiment Volunteers, with its vaunted battery, of six 13-pounder rifle guns. Sloan's companies were then brought into action, having been pushed forward through the woods. The enemy, soon galled and staggered by the fire, and pressed by the determined valor, with which Wheat handled his battalion, until he was desperately wounded, hastened up three other regiments of the brigade and two Dahlgreen howitzers, making in all quite 3,500 bayonets, and eight pieces of artillery, opposed to less than 800 men, and two 6-pounder guns.

Despite this odds, this intrepid command, of but eleven weak companies, maintained its front to the enemy for quite an hour, and until General Bee came to their aid with his command. The heroic Bee, with a soldier's eye and recognition of the situation, had previously disposed his command with skill—Imboden's battery having been admirably placed between the two brigades, under shelter, behind the undulations of a hill about 150 yards north of the now famous Henry House, and very near where he subsequently fell, mortally wounded, to the great misfortune of his country, but after deeds of deliberate and ever memorable courage.

Meanwhile, the enemy had pushed forward a battalion of eight companies of regular infantry, and one of their best batteries, of six pieces, (four rifled), supported by four companies of marines, to increase the desperate odds against which Evans and his men had maintained their stand, with an almost matchless tenacity.

General Bee, now finding Evans sorely pressed, under the crushing weight of the masses of the enemy, at the call of Colonel Evans, threw forward his whole force to his aid across a small stream—Young's Branch and Valley—and engaged the Federalists with impetuosity; Imboden's Battery at the time playing from his well chosen position with brilliant effect with spherical case, the enemy having first opened on him from a rifle battery, probably Griffin's, with elongated cylindrical shells, which flew a few feet over the heads of our men, and exploded in the crest of the hill immediately in rear.

As Bee advanced under a severe fire, he placed the 7th and 8th Georgia Regiments, under the chivalrous Bartow, at about 11, A. M., in a wood of second-growth pines to the right and front of, and nearly perpendicular to Evans's line of battle; the 4th Alabama to the left of them, along a fence connecting the position of the Georgia Regiments with the rectangular copse in which Sloan's South Carolina companies were engaged, and into which, he also threw the 2nd Mississippi. A fierce and destructive conflict now ensued—the fire was withering on both sides, while the enemy swept our short, thin lines with their numerous artillery, which, according to their official reports, at this time consisted of at least ten rifle guns and four howitzers. For an hour, did these stout-hearted men of the blended commands of Bee, Evans and Bartow, breast an unintermitting battle-storm, animated surely, by something more than the ordinary courage of even the bravest men under fire; it must have been, indeed, the inspiration of the cause, and consciousness of the great stake at issue, which thus nerved and animated one and all, to stand unawed and unshrinking in such extremity.

Two Federal Brigades, of Heintzleman's Division, were now brought into action, led by Ricketts's superb light Battery, of six 10-pounder rifle guns, which, posted on an eminence to the right of the Sudley Road, opened fire on Imboden's Battery—about this time increased by two rifle pieces of the Washington Artillery, under Lieut. Richardson, and already the mark of two batteries, which divided their fire with Imboden, and two guns, under Lieutenants Davidson and Leftwitch, of Latham's Battery, posted as before mentioned.

At this time, confronting the enemy, we had still but Evans's eleven companies and two guns—Bee's and Bartow's four regiments, the two companies 11th Mississippi, under Lieut. Col. Liddell, and the six pieces, under Imboden and Richardson. The enemy had two divisions, of four strong brigades, including seventeen companies of regular infantry, cavalry and artillery, four companies of marines, and twenty pieces of artillery.* Against this odds, scarcely credible, our advance position was still for a while maintained, and the enemy's ranks constantly broken

---

* See Official Reports of Colonels Heintzleman, Porter, &c.

and shattered under the scorching fire of our men; but fresh regiments of the Federalists came upon the field, Sherman's and Keye's Brigades, of Tyler's Division, as is stated in their reports, numbering over 6,000 bayonets, which had found a passage across the Run, about 800 yards above the Stone Bridge, threatened our right.

Heavy losses had now been sustained on our side, both in numbers and in the personal worth of the slain. The 8th Georgia Regiment had suffered heavily, being exposed as it took and maintained its position, to a fire from the enemy, already posted within a hundred yards of their front and right, sheltered by fences and other cover. It was at this time that Lieut. Col. Gardner was severely wounded, as also several other valuable officers; the Adjutant of the Regiment, Lieut. Branch, was killed, and the horse of the regretted Bartow was shot under him. The 4th Alabama also suffered severely from the deadly fire of the thousands of muskets which they so dauntlessly affronted under the immediate leadership of Bee himself. Its brave Colonel, E. J. Jones, was dangerously wounded, and many gallant officers fell, slain, or *hors de combat*.

Now, however, with the surging mass of over fourteen thousand Federal infantry, pressing on their front and under the incessant fire of at least twenty pieces of artillery, with the fresh Brigades of Sherman and Keye's approaching—the latter already in musket range—our lines gave back, but under orders from Gen. Bee.

The enemy, maintaining their fire, pressed their swelling masses onward as our shattered battalions retired; the slaughter for the moment was deplorable, and has filled many a Southern home with life-long sorrow.

Under this inexorable stress, the retreat continued, until arrested by the energy and resolution of Gen. Bee, supported by Bartow and Evans, just in rear of the Robinson House, and Hampton's Legion which had been already advanced, and was in position near it.

Imboden's Battery, which had been handled with marked skill, but whose men were almost exhausted, and the two pieces of Walton's Battery, under Lieut. Richardson, being threatened by the enemy's infantry on the left and front, were also obliged to fall back—Imboden leaving a disabled piece on the ground retired until he met Jackson's Brigade, while Richardson joined the main body of his battery near the Lewis House.

As our infantry retired from the extreme front, the two six-pounders of Latham's Battery, before mentioned, fell back with excellent judgment to suitable positions in the rear, whence an effective fire was maintained upon the still advancing lines of the Federalists, with damaging effect, until their ammunition was nearly exhausted, when they, too, were withdrawn in the near presence of the enemy, and rejoined their captain.

From the point, previously indicated, where General Johnston and myself had established our headquarters, we heard the continuous roll of musketry, and the sustained din of the artillery, which announced the serious outburst of the battle on our left flank, and we anxiously, but confidently, awaited similar sounds of conflict from our front at Centreville, resulting from the prescribed attack in that quarter, by our right wing.

At half past ten, A. M., however, this expectation was dissipated by a dispatch from Brig. Gen. Ewell, informing me, to my profound disappointment, that my orders for his advance had miscarried, but, that in consequence of a communication from General D. R. Jones, he had just thrown his brigade across the stream at Union Mills. But, in my judgment, it was now too late for the effective execution of the contemplated movement, which must have required quite three hours for the troops to get into position for the attack. Therefore, it became immediately necessary to depend on new combinations, and other dispositions suited to the now pressing exigency. The movement of the right and centre, already begun by Jones and Longstreet, was at once countermanded, with the sanction of General Johnston, and we arranged to meet the enemy on the field upon which he had chosen to give us battle. Under these circumstances, our reserves, not already in movement, were immediately ordered up to support our left flank, namely: Holmes's two regiments, and battery of artillery, under Captain Lindsey Walker, of six guns, and Earley's Brigade. Two regiments from Bonham's brigade, with Kemper's four six-pounders were also called for, and, with the sanction of General Johnston, Generals Ewell, Jones, (D. R.,) Longstreet and Bonham were directed to make a demonstration to their several fronts to retain and engross the enemy's reserves and any forces on their flank, and at and around Centreville. Previously, our respective Chiefs of Staff, Major Rhett and Colonel Jordan, had been left at my headquarters to hasten up, and give directions to any troops that might arrive at Manassas.

These orders having been duly dispatched by staff

officers at 11.30, A. M., General Johnston and myself set out for the immediate field of action, which we reached in rear of the Robinson and Widow Henry's Houses, at about 12 meridian, and just as the commands of Bee, Bartow and Evans, had taken shelter in a wooded ravine behind the former, stoutly held at the time by Hampton with his Legion, which had made a stand there after having previously been as far forward as the Turnpike, where Lieutenant Colonel Johnston, an officer of brilliant promise, was killed, and other severe losses were sustained.

Before our arrival upon the scene, General Jackson had moved forward with his Brigade, of five Virginia regiments, from his position in reserve, and had judiciously taken post below the brim of the plateau, nearly east of the Henry House, and to the left of the ravine and woods occupied by the mingled remnants of Bee's, Bartow's and Evans's command, with Imboden's Battery, and two of Stanard's pieces, placed so as to play upon the on-coming enemy, supported in the immediate rear by Colonel J. L. Preston's and Lieut. Colonel Echols's Regiments, on the right by Harper's, and on the left by Allen's and Cummings's Regiment.

As soon as General Johnston and myself reached the field, we were occupied with the reorganization of the heroic troops, whose previous stand, with scarce a parallel, has nothing more valiant in all the pages of history, and whose losses fitly tell why, at length, their ranks had lost their cohesion. It was now that General Johnston, impressively and gallantly charged to the front, with the colors of the Fourth Alabama Regiment by his side, all the field officers of the regiment having been previously disabled. Shortly afterwards I placed S. R. Gist, Adjutant and Inspector General of South Carolina, a volunteer Aid of General Bee, in command of this regiment, and who led it again to the front as became its previous behavior, and remained with it for the rest of the day.

As soon as we had thus rallied and disposed our forces, I urged General Johnston to leave the immediate conduct of the field to me, while he, repairing to Portici—the Lewis House—should urge reinforcements forward. At first he was unwilling, but reminded that one of us must do so, and that, properly, it was his place, he reluctantly, but fortunately, complied; fortunately, because from that position, by his energy and sagacity, his keen perception and anticipation of my needs, he so directed the reserves as to ensure the success of the day.

As General Johnston departed for Portici, Colonel Bartow reported to me with the remains of the Seventh Georgia volunteers—Gartrell's—which I ordered him to post on the left of Jackson's line, in the edge of the belt of pines bordering the south-eastern rim of the plateau, on which the battle was now to rage so long and so fiercely.

Col. Wm. Smith's Battalion of the 49th Virginia Volunteers, having also come up by my orders, I placed it on the left of Gartrell's as my extreme left at the time. Repairing then to the right, I placed Hampton's Legion, which had suffered greatly, on that flank, somewhat to the rear of Harper's Regiment, and also the seven companies, of the 8th (Hunton's) Virginia Regiment, which, detached from Cocke's Brigade, by my orders, and those of Gen. Johnston, had opportunely reached the ground. These, with Harper's Regiment, constituted a reserve, to protect our right flank from an advance of the enemy from the quarter of the Stone Bridge, and served as a support for the line of battle, which was formed on the right by Bee's and Evans's commands, in the centre by four regiments of Jackson's Brigade, with Imboden's four six-pounders, Walton's five guns (two rifled,) two guns (one piece rifled) of Stanard's and two six-pounders, of Rogers's Batteries, the latter under Lt. Heaton; and on the left by Gartrell's reduced ranks and Col. Smith's battalion, subsequently reinforced by Falkner's Second Mississippi Regiment, and by another regiment of the Army of Shenandoah, just arrived upon the field, the Sixth (Fisher's) North Carolina. Confronting the enemy at this time, my forces numbered, at most, not more than 6,500 infantry and artillerists, with but thirteen pieces of artillery, and two companies (Carter's and Hoge's) of Stuart's cavalry.

The enemy's force, now bearing hotly and confidently down on our position—regiment after regiment of the best equipped men that ever took the field—according to their own official history of the day, was formed of Colonels Hunter's and Heintzelman's Divisions, Colonels Sherman's and Keyes's Brigades, of Tyler's Division, and of the formidable batteries of Ricketts, Griffin and Arnold regulars, and Second Rhode Island, and two Dahlgreen howitzers—a force of over 20,000 infantry, seven companies of regular cavalry, and twenty-four pieces of improved artillery. At the same time, perilous, heavy reserves of infantry and artillery hung in the distance around the Stone Bridge, Mitchell's, Blackburn's and Union Mills' Fords, visibly ready to fall upon us at any moment; and I was also assured of the existence of other heavy corps, at and around

Centreville and elsewhere, within convenient supporting distances.

Fully conscious of this portentous disparity of force, as I posted the lines for the encounter, I sought to infuse into the hearts of my officers and men, the confidence and determined spirit of resistance to this wicked invasion of the homes of a free people, which I felt. I informed them that reinforcements would rapidly come to their support, and that we must, at all hazards, hold our posts until reinforced. I reminded them that we fought for our homes, our firesides, and for the independence of our country. I urged them to the resolution of victory or death on that field. These sentiments were loudly, eagerly cheered, wheresoever proclaimed, and I then felt reassured of the unconquerable spirit of that army, which would enable us to wrench victory from the host then threatening us with destruction.

Oh, my country! I would readily have sacrificed my life and those of all the brave men around me, to save your honor, and to maintain your independence from the degrading yoke which those ruthless invaders had come to impose and render perpetual, and the day's issue has assured me, that such emotions must also have animated all under my command.

In the meantime, the enemy had seized upon the plateau, on which Robinson's and the Henry Houses are situated—the position first occupied in the morning by Gen. Bee, before advancing to the support of Evans—Ricketts' Battery, of six rifle guns, the pride of the Federalists, the object of their unstinted expenditure in outfit, and the equally powerful Regular Light Battery, of Griffin, were brought forward and placed in immediate action, after having, conjointly with the batteries already mentioned, played from former positions with destructive effect upon our forward battalions.

The topographical features of the plateau, now become the stage of the contending armies, must be described in outline.

A glance at the map, will show that it is enclosed on three sides by small water courses, which empty into Bull Run within a few yards of each other, a half-a-mile to the south of the Stone Bridge. Rising to an elevation of quite one hundred feet above the level of Bull Run at the Bridge, it falls off on three sides to the level of the enclosing streams in gentle slopes, but which are furrowed by ravines of irregular direction and length, and studded with clumps and patches of young pines and oaks. The general direction of the crest of the plateau, is oblique to the course of Bull Run in that quarter, and to the Brentsville and Turnpike Roads which intersect each other at right angles. Immediately surrounding the two houses, before mentioned, are small open fields of irregular outline, not exceeding 150 acres in extent. The houses occupied at the time, the one by the Widow Henry and the other by the free negro Robinson, are small wooden buildings, the latter densely embowered in trees, and environed by a double row of fences on two sides. Around the eastern and southern brow of the plateau, an almost unbroken fringe of second-growth pines, gave excellent shelter for our marksmen, who availed themselves of it with the most satisfactory skill. To the west, adjoining the fields, a broad belt of oaks extends directly across the crest on both sides of the Sudley Road, in which, during the battle, regiments of both armies met and contended for the mastery.

From the open ground of this plateau the view embraces a wide expanse of woods, and gently undulating, open country of broad grass and grain fields in all directions, including the scene of Evans and Bee's recent encounter with the enemy, some 1,200 yards to the northward.

In reply to the play of the enemy's batteries our own artillery had not been either idle or unskillful. The ground occupied by our guns, on a level with that held by the batteries of the enemy, was an open space, of limited extent, behind a low undulation, just at the eastern verge of the plateau, some 500 or 600 yards from the Henry House. Here, as before said, 13 pieces, mostly six-pounders, were maintained in action. The several batteries of Imboden, Stanard, Pendleton, (Rockbridge Artillery), and Alburtis's, of the Army of the Shenandoah, and five guns of Walton's, and Heaton's section of Rogers's Battery, of the Army of the Potomac, alternating, to some extent, with each other, and taking part as needed: all from the outset displaying that marvellous capacity of our people, as artillerists, which has made them, it would appear, at once the terror and the admiration of the enemy.

As was soon apparent, the Federalists had suffered severely from our artillery, and from the fire of our musketry on the right, and especially from the left flank, placed under cover, within whose galling range they had been advanced. And we are told in their official reports, how regiment after regiment, thrown forward to dislodge us, was broken, never to recover its entire organization on that field.

In the meantime, also, two companies of Stuart's cavalry (Carter's and Hoge's), made a dashing charge down the Brentsville and Sudley road upon the Fire Zouaves—then the enemy's right on the plateau—which added to their disorder, wrought by our musketry, on that flank. But still, the press of the enemy was heavy in that quarter of the field, as fresh troops were thrown forward there to outflank us; and some three guns of a battery, in an attempt to obtain a position, apparently to enfilade our batteries, were thrown so close to the 33d Regiment, Jackson's Brigade, that that regiment, springing forward, seized them, but with severe loss, and was subsequently driven back by an overpowering force of Federal musketry.

Now, full 2 o'clock, P. M., I gave the order for the right of my line, except my reserves, to advance to recover the plateau. It was done with uncommon resolution and vigor, and at the same time Jackson's Brigade pierced the enemy's centre with the determination of veterans, and the spirit of men who fight for a sacred cause; but it suffered seriously. With equal spirit the other parts of the line made the onset, and the Federal lines were broken and swept back at all points from the open ground of the plateau. Rallying soon, however, as they were strongly reinforced by fresh regiments, the Federalists returned, and by weight of numbers, pressed our lines back, recovered their ground and guns, and renewed the offensive.

By this time, between half-past 2 and 3 o'clock, P. M., our reinforcements pushed forward, and directed by General Johnston to the required quarter, were at hand just as I had ordered forward, to a second effort, for the recovery of the disputed plateau, the whole line, including my reserve, which, at this crisis of the battle, I felt called upon to lead in person. This attack was general, and was share l in by every regiment then in the field, including the 6th, Fisher's North Carolina regiment, which had just come up and taken position on the immediate left of the 49th Virginia Regiment. The whole open ground was again swept clear of the enemy, and the plateau around the Henry and Robinson Houses remained finally in our possession, with the greater part of the Ricketts and Griffin batteries, and a flag of the 1st Michigan Regiment, captured by the 27th Virginia Regiment, (Lieut. Col. Echols,) of Jackson's Brigade. This part of the day was rich with deeds of individual coolness and dauntless conduct, as well as well-directed, embodied resolution and bravery, but fraught with the loss to the service of the country, of lives of inestimable preciousness at this juncture. The brave Bee was mortally wounded at the head of the 4th Alabama and some Mississippians, in the open field near the Henry House; and a few yards distant, the promising life of Bartow, while leading the 7th Georgia Regiment, was quenched in blood. Colonel F. J. Thomas, Acting Chief of Ordnance, of Gen. Johnston's Staff, after gallant conduct and most efficient service, was also slain. Col. Fisher—6th North Carolina—likewise fell, after soldierly behavior at the head of his regiment, with ranks greatly thinned.

Withers's 18th Regiment, of Cocke's Brigade, had come up in time to follow this charge, and in conjunction with Hampton's Legion, captured several rifle pieces, which may have fallen previously in possession of some of our troops; but, if so, had been recovered by the enemy. These pieces were immediately turned, and effectively served on distant masses of the enemy, by the hands of some of our officers.

While the enemy had thus been driven back on our right, entirely across the turnpike and beyond Young's Branch, on our left, the woods yet swarmed with them, when our reinforcements opportunely arrived in quick succession, and took position in that portion of the field. Kershaw's 2nd and Cash's 8th South Carolina Regiments, which had arrived soon after Withers's, were led through the oaks just east of the Sudley-Brentsville Road, brushing some of the enemy before them, and taking an advantageous position along and west of that road, opened with much skill and effect on bodies of the enemy that had been rallied under cover of a strong Federal brigade, posted on a plateau in the southwest angle, formed by intersection of the Turnpike with the S.-B. Road. Among the troops thus engaged, were the Federal regular infantry.

At the same time, Kemper's Battery, passing northward by the S.-B. Road, took position on the open space—under orders of Colonel Kershaw—near where an enemy's battery had been captured, and was opened with effective results upon the Federal right, then the mark also of Kershaw and Cash's Regiments.

Preston's 28th Regiment, of Cocke's Brigade, had by that time, entered the same body of oaks, and encountered some Michigan troops, capturing their Brigade Commander, Col. Wilcox.

Another important accession to our forces had also occurred about the same time, 3 o'clock, P. M. Brigadier Gen. E. K. Smith, with some 1,700 infantry of Elzey's Brigade, of the Army of the Shenandoah, and Beckham's Battery, came upon the field, from Camp Pickens, Manassas, where they had arrived by railroad at noon. Directed in person by Gen. Johnston, to the left, then so much endangered, on reaching a position in rear of the oak woods, south of the Henry House, and immediately east of the Sudley Road, Gen. Smith was disabled by a severe wound, and his valuable services were lost at that critical juncture. But the command devolved upon a meritorious officer of experience—Col. Elzey—who led his infantry at once somewhat further to the left, in the direction of the Chinn House, across the road, through the oaks skirting the west side of the road, and around which he sent the battery under Lieut. Beckham. This officer took up a most favorable position near that house, whence, with a clear view of the Federal right and centre, filling the open fields to the west of the Brentsville-Sudley Road, and gently sloping southward, he opened fire with his battery upon them with deadly and damaging effect.

Col. Early, who, by some mischance, did not receive orders until 2 o'clock, which had been sent him at noon, came on the ground immediately after Elzey, with Kemper's 7th Virginia, Hays's 7th Louisiana, and Barksdale's 13th Mississippi regiments. This Brigade, by the personal direction of General Johnston, was marched by the Holkham House, across the fields to the left, entirely around the woods through which Elzey had passed, and under a severe fire, into a position in line of battle near Chinn's House, outflanking the enemy's right.

At this time, about 3.30, P. M., the enemy driven back on their left and centre, and brushed from the woods bordering the Sudley Road, south and west of the Henry House, had formed a line of battle of truly formidable proportions, of crescent outline, reaching on their left, from vicinity of Pittsylvania, (the old Carter Mansion), by Matthew's and in rear of Dogan's, across the Turnpike near to Chinn's House. The woods and fields were filled with their masses of infantry and their carefully preserved cavalry. It was a truly magnificent, though redoubtable spectacle, as they threw forward in fine style, on the broad gentle slopes of the ridge occupied by their main lines, a cloud of skirmishers, preparatory for another attack.

But as Early formed his line, and Beckham's pieces played upon the right of the enemy, Elzey's Brigade, Gibbon's 10th Virginia, Lieut. Colonel Stuart's 1st Maryland, and Vaughan's 3d Tennessee Regiments, and Cash's 8th and Kershaw's 2d South Carolina, Withers's 18th and Preston's 28th Virginia, advanced in an irregular line, almost simultaneously, with great spirit from their several positions, upon the front and flanks of the enemy, in their quarter of the field. At the same time, too, Early resolutely assailed their right flank and rear. Under this combined attack, the enemy was soon forced, first over the narrow plateau in the southern angle made by the two roads so often mentioned, into a patch of woods on its western slope, thence back over Young's Branch and the Turnpike, into the fields of the Dogan Farm, and rearward in extreme disorder, in all available directions, towards Bull Run. The rout had now become general and complete.

About the time that Elzey and Early were entering into action, a column of the enemy, Keyes's Brigade of Tyler's Division, made its way across the Turnpike between Bull Run and the Robinson House, under cover of a wood and brow of the ridges, apparently to turn my right, but was easily repulsed by a few shots from Latham's Battery, now united and placed in position by Captain D. B. Harris, of the Virginia Engineers, whose services during the day became his character as an able, cool and skillful officer; and from Alburtis's Battery, opportunely ordered, by General Jackson, to a position to the right of Latham, on a hill commanding the line of approach of the enemy, and supported by portions of regiments collected together by the Staff Officers of General Johnston and myself.

Early's Brigade, meanwhile, joined by the 19th Virginia Regiment, Lieutenant-Colonel Strange, of Cocke's Brigade, pursued the now panic-stricken, fugitive enemy. Stuart, with his cavalry, and Beckham, had also taken up the pursuit along the road by which the enemy had come upon the field that morning; but soon, cumbered by prisoners who thronged his way, the former was unable to attack the mass of the fast-fleeing, frantic Federalists. Withers's, R. T. Preston's, Cash's and Kershaw's Regiments, Hampton's Legion and Kemper's Battery also pursued along the Warrenton road by the Stone Bridge, the enemy having opportunely opened a way for them through the heavy abatis which my troops had made on the west side of the bridge several days before. But this pursuit was soon recalled, in consequence of a false report which unfortunately reached us, that the enemy's reserves, known to be fresh and of considerable strength, were threatening the position of Union Mills Ford.

Colonel Radford, with six companies Virginia cavalry, was also ordered by General Johnston to cross Bull Run and attack the enemy from the direction of

Lewis's House; conducted by one of my Aids, Colonel Chisholm, by the Lewis Ford, to the immediate vicinity of the Suspension Bridge, he charged a battery with great gallantry, took Colonel Corcoran, of the 69th regiment New York Volunteers, a prisoner, and captured the Federal colors of that regiment, as well as a number of the enemy. He lost, however, a promising officer of his regiment, Captain Winston Radford.

Lieutenant-Colonel Munford also led some companies of cavalry in hot pursuit, and rendered material service in the capture of prisoners and of cannon, horses, ammunition, &c., abandoned by the enemy in their flight.

Captain Lay's company of the Powhatan troops, and Utterback's Rangers, Virginia volunteers, attached to my person, did material service, under Captain Lay, in rallying troops broken for the time by the onset of the enemy's masses.

During the period of the momentous events fraught with the weal of our country, which were passing on the blood-stained plateau along the Sudley and Warrenton Roads, other portions of the line of Bull Run had not been void of action of moment and of influence upon the general result.

While Colonel Evans and his sturdy band were holding at bay the Federal advance beyond the Turnpike, the enemy made repeated demonstrations, with artillery and infantry, upon the line of Cocke's Brigade, with the serious intention of forcing the position, as General Schenck admits in his report. They were driven back with severe loss by Latham's (a section) and Rogers's four six-pounders, and were so impressed with the strength of that line as to be held in check and inactive, even after it had been stripped of all its troops but one company of the 19th Virginia Regiment, under Captain Duke, a meritorious officer. And it is worthy of notice that, in this encounter of our six-pounder guns, handled by our volunteer artillerists, they had worsted such a notorious adversary as the Ayres's—formerly Sherman's—Battery, which quit the contest under the illusion that it had weightier metal than its own to contend with.

The centre Brigades—Bonham's and Longstreet's—of the line of Bull Run, if not closely engaged, were nevertheless exposed for much of the day to an annoying, almost incessant fire of artillery of long range; but, by a steady, veteran-like maintenance of their positions, they held, virtually paralyzed all day, two strong brigades of the enemy, with their batteries (four) of rifle guns.

As before said, two regiments of Bonham's Brigade, 2nd and 8th South Carolina volunteers, and Kemper's Battery, took a distinguished part in the battle. The remainder, 3rd Williams's. 7th Bacon's South Carolina volunteers; 11th (Kirkland's) North Carolina Regiment; six companies 8th Louisiana volunteers; Shield's Battery, and one section of Walton's Battery under Lieutentant Garnett, whether in holding their post or taking up the pursuit, officers and men, discharged their duty with credit and promise.

Longstreet's Brigade, pursuant to orders prescribing his part of the operations of the centre and right wing, was thrown across Bull Run early in the morning, and under a severe fire of artillery, was skillfully disposed for the assault of the enemy's batteries in that quarter, but were withdrawn subsequently, in consequence of the change of plan already mentioned and explained. The troops of this brigade were, 1st, Major Skinner; 11th, Garland's; 24th, Lieutenant-Colonel Hairston; 17th, Corse, Virginia Regiments; 5th North Carolina, Lieutenant-Colonel Jones, and Whitehead's company Virginia cavalry. Throughout the day these troops evinced the most soldierly spirit.

After the rout, having been ordered by General Johnston in the direction of Centreville in pursuit, these brigades advanced near to that place, when night and darkness intervening, General Bonham thought it proper to direct his own brigade and that of General Longstreet back to Bull Run.

General D. R. Jones early in the day crossing Bull Run with his brigade, pursuant to orders, indicating his part in the projected attack by our right wing and centre on the enemy at Centreville, took up a position on the Union Mills and Centreville Road, more than a mile in advance of the Run. Ordered back, in consequence of the miscarriage of the orders to General Ewell, the retrograde movement was necessarily made under a sharp fire of artillery.

At noon this brigade, in obedience to new instructions, was again thrown across Bull Run to make demonstrations. Unsupported by other troops, the advance was gallantly made until within musket range of the enemy's force—Colonel Davies' Brigade, in position near Rocky Run, and under the concentrated fire of their artillery. In this affair the 5th, Jenkins's South Carolina, and Captain Fountaine's company of the 18th Mississippi Regiment are mentioned by General Jones as having shown conspicuous gallantry, coolness and discipline, under a combined fire of infantry and artillery. Not only did the return fire of the brigade drive to cover the enemy's infantry, but the movement unquestionably spread through the enemy's ranks a sense of insecurity and danger from an attack by that route on their rear at Centreville, which served to augment the extraordinary panic which we know disbanded the entire Federal Army for the time. This is evident from the fact that Colonel Davies, the immediate adversary's commander, in his official report was induced to magnify one small company of our cavalry, which accompanied the brigade, into a force of 2,000 men; and Colonel Miles, the commander of the Federal Reserves at Centreville, says the movement "caused painful apprehensions for the left flank" of their army.

General Ewell, occupying for the time the right of the lines of Bull Run at Union Mills Ford, after the miscarriage of my orders for his advance upon Centreville, in the afternoon, was ordered by General Johnston to bring up his brigade into battle then raging on the left flank. Promptly executed as this movement was, the brigade, after a severe march, reached the field too late to share the glories, as they had the labors, of the day. As the important position at the Union Mills had been left with but a slender guard, General Ewell was at once ordered to retrace his steps and resume his position to prevent the possibility of its seizure by any force of the enemy in that quarter.

Brigadier General Holmes—left with his brigade as a support to the same position in the original plan of battle—had also been called to the left, whither he marched with the utmost speed, but not in time to join actively in the battle.

Walker's rifle guns of the brigade, however, came

up in time to be fired with precision and decided execution at the retreating enemy, and Scott's cavalry, joining in the pursuit, assisted in the capture of prisoners and war munitions.

This victory, the details of which I have thus sought to chronicle as fully as were fitting an official report, it remains to record, was dearly won by the death of many officers and men of inestimable value, belonging to all grades of our society.

In the death of General Barnard E. Bee the Confederacy has sustained an irreparable loss, for with great personal bravery and coolness, he possessed the qualities of an accomplished soldier, and an able, reliable commander.

Colonels Bartow and Fisher, and Lieutenant Colonel Johnson of Hampton's Legion, in the fearless command of their men, gave earnest of great usefulness to the service, had they been spared to complete a career so brilliantly begun. Besides the field officers, already mentioned as having been wounded while in the gallant discharge of their duties, many others also received severe wounds after equally honorable and distinguished conduct, whether in leading their men forward, or in rallying them, when overpowered or temporarily shattered by the largely superior force, to which we were generally opposed.

The subordinate grades were likewise abundantly conspicuous for zeal and capacity for the leadership of men in arms. To mention all, who, fighting well, paid the lavish forfeit of their lives, or at least crippled, mutilated bodies on the field of Manassas, cannot well be done within the compass of this paper, but a grateful country and mourning friends will not suffer their names and services to be forgotten, and pass away unhonored.

Nor are those officers and men who were so fortunate as to escape the thick-flying, deadly missiles, of the enemy, less worthy of praise for their endurance, firmness and valor than their brothers-in-arms, whose lives were closed, or bodies maimed, on that memorable day. To mention all who exhibited ability and brilliant courage, were impossible in this report; nor do the reports of Brigade and other subordinate commanders, supply full lists of all actually deserving of distinction. I can only mention those whose conduct came immediately under my notice, or the consequence of whose actions happened to be signally important.

It is fit that I should, in this way, commend to notice the dauntless conduct and imperturbable coolness of Col. Evans; and well indeed was he supported by Col. Sloan and the officers of the Fourth South Carolina Regiment, as also, Major Wheat, than whom, no one displayed more brilliant courage until carried from the field, shot through the lungs; though happily, not mortally stricken. But in the desperately unequal contest, to which those brave gentlemen were, for a time, necessarily exposed, the behavior of officers and men generally, was worthy of the highest admiration; and assuredly, hereafter, all there present, may proudly say: We were of that band who fought the first hour of the battle of Manassas. Equal honors and credit must also be awarded in the pages of history, to the gallant officers and men, who, under Bee and Bartow, subsequently marching to their side, saved them from destruction, and relieved them from the brunt of the enemy's attack.

The conduct of Gen. Jackson also requires mention as eminently that of an able, fearless soldier, and sagacious commander, one fit to lead his efficient brigade: his prompt, timely arrival before the plateau of the Henry House, and his judicious disposition of his troops contributed much to the success of the day. Although painfully wounded in the hand, he remained on the field to the end of the battle, rendering invaluable assistance.

Col. Wm. Smith was as efficient, as self-possessed and brave; the influence of his example and his words of encouragement was not confined to his immediate command, the good conduct of which is especially noticeable, inasmuch as it had been embodied but a day or two before the battle.

Colonels Harper, Hunton and Hampton, commanding regiments of the reserve, attracted my notice, by their soldierly ability, as with their gallant commands, they restored the fortunes of the day, at a time when the enemy, by a last desperate onset, with heavy odds, had driven our forces from the fiercely contested ground around the Henry and Robinson Houses. Veterans could not have behaved better than these well led regiments.

High praise must also be given to Colonels Cocke, Early and Elzey, Brigade Commanders; also, to Col. Kershaw, commanding, for the time, the Second and Eighth South Carolina Regiments. Under the instructions of General Johnston, these officers reached the field at an opportune, critical moment, and disposed, handled and fought their respective commands, with sagacity, decision and successful results, which have been described in detail.

Col. J. E. B. Stuart likewise deserves mention, for his enterprise and ability as a cavalry commander,

Through his judicious reconnoisance of the country on our left flank, he acquired information, both of topographical features and the positions of the enemy, of the utmost importance in the subsequent and closing movements of the day on that flank, and his services in the pursuit, were highly effective.

Capt. E. P. Alexander, C. S. Engineers, gave me seasonable and material assistance early in the day, with his system of signals. Almost the first shot fired by the enemy passed through the tent of his party at the Stone Bridge, where they subsequently firmly maintained their position in the discharge of their duty—the transmission of messages of the enemy's movements—for several hours under fire. Later, Captain Alexander acted as my Aid-de-Camp, in the transmission of orders, and in observation of the enemy.

I was most efficiently served throughout the day by my Volunteer Aids, Colonels Preston, Manning, Chesnut, Miles, Rice, Heyward and Chisholm, to whom I tender my thanks for their unflagging, intelligent and fearless discharge of the laborious, responsible duties entrusted to them. To Lieut. S. W. Ferguson, A. D. C., and Col. Heyward, who were habitually at my side, from 12 noon until the close of the battle; my special acknowledgments are due. The horse of the former was killed under him by the same shell that wounded that of the latter. Both were eminently useful to me, and were distinguished for coolness and courage, until the enemy gave way and fled in wild disorder in every direction— a scene the President of the Confederacy had the high satisfaction of witnessing, as he arrived upon the field at that exultant moment.

I also received, from the time I reached the front,

such signal service from H. E. Peyton, at the time a private in the Loudoun cavalry, that I have called him to my personal staff. Similar services were also rendered me, repeatedly during the battle, by T. J. Randolph, a Volunteer Acting A. D. C. to Colonel Cocke.

Captain Clifton H. Smith, of the General Staff, was also present on the field, and rendered efficient service in the transmission of orders.

It must be permitted me here, to record my profound sense of my obligations to General Johnston, for his generous permission to carry out my plans, with such modifications as circumstances had required. From his services on the field, as we entered it together, already mentioned, and his subsequent watchful management of the reinforcements as they reached the vicinity of the field, our countrymen may draw the most auspicious auguries.

To Colonel Thomas Jordan, my efficient and zealous Assistant Adjutant-General, much credit is due for his able assistance in the organization of the forces under my command and for the intelligence and promptness with which he has discharged all the laborious and important duties of his office.

Valuable assistance was given to me by Major Cabell, chief officer of the Quartermaster's Department, in the sphere of his duties—duties environed by far more than the ordinary difficulties and embarrassments attending the operations of a long organized, regular establishment.

Colonel R. B. Lee, Chief of Subsistence Department, had but just entered upon his duties, but his experience, and long and varied services in his department, made him as efficient as possible.

Captain W. H. Fowle, whom Colonel Lee had relieved, had previously exerted himself to the utmost to carry out orders from these headquarters, to render his department equal to the demands of the service; that it was not entirely so, it is due to justice to say, was certainly not his fault.

Deprived, by the sudden severe illness, of the Medical Director, Surgeon Thomas H. Williams, his duties were discharged by Surgeon R. L. Brodie, to my entire satisfaction; and it is proper to say, that the entire medical corps of the army at present, embracing gentlemen of distinction in the profession, who had quit lucrative private practice, by their services in the field and subsequently, did high honor to their profession.

The vital duties of the Ordnance Department were effectively discharged under the administration of my Chief of Artillery and Ordnance, Colonel Samuel Jones.

At one time, when reports of evil omen and disaster reached Camp Pickens, with such circumstantiality as to give reasonable grounds of anxiety, its commander, Colonel Terrett, the commander of the entrenched batteries, Captain Sterrett, of the Confederate States Navy, and their officers, made the most efficient possible preparations for the desperate defence of that position in extremity; and in this connection, I regret my inability to mention the names of those patriotic gentlemen of Virginia, by the gratuitous labor of whose slaves the entrenched camp at Manassas had been mainly constructed, relieving the troops from that laborious service, and giving opportunity for their military instruction.

Lieutenant-Colonel Thomas H. Williamson, the Engineer of these works, assisted by Captain D. B.

Harris, discharged his duties with untiring energy and devotion, as well as satisfactory skill.

Captain W. H. Stevens, Engineer Confederate States Army, served with the advanced forces at Fairfax Court-House for some time before the battle; he laid out the works there, in admirable accordance with the purposes for which they were designed, and yet so as to admit of ultimate extension and adaptation to more serious uses as means and part of a system of real defence when determined upon. He has shown himself to be an officer of energy and ability.

Major Thomas G. Rhett, after having discharged for several months the laborious duties of Adjutant-General to the commanding officer of Camp Pickens, was detached to join the Army of the Shenandoah, just on the eve of the advance of the enemy, but volunteering his services, was ordered to assist on the Staff of General Bonham, joining that officer at Centreville on the night of the 17th, before the battle of Bull Run, where he rendered valuable services, until the arrival of General Johnston, on the 20th of July, when he was called to the place of Chief of Staff of that officer.

It is also proper to acknowledge the signal services rendered by Colonel B. F. Terry and T. Lubbock, of Texas, who had attached themselves to the staff of General Longstreet. These gentlemen made daring and valuable reconnoisances of the enemy's positions, assisted by Captains Goree and Chichester; they also carried orders in the field, and on the following day, accompanying Captain Whitehead's troop to take possession of Fairfax Court-House, Colonel Terry, with his unerring rifle, severed the halliard, and thus lowered the Federal flag found still floating from the cupola of the Court-House there. He also secured a large Federal garrison flag, designed, it is said, to be unfurled over our entrenchments at Manassas.

In connection with the unfortunate casualty of the day—that is, the miscarriage of the orders sent by courier to Generals Holmes and Ewell to attack the enemy in flank and reverse at Centreville, through which the triumph of our arms was prevented from being still more decisive, I regard it in place to say, a divisional organization, with officers in command of divisions, with appropriate rank, as in European services, would greatly reduce the risk of such mishaps, and would advantageously simplify the communications of a General in command of a field with his troops.

While glorious for our people, and of crushing effect upon the *morale* of our hitherto confident and over-weening adversary, as were the events of the battle of Manassas, the field was only won by stout fighting, and, as before reported, with much loss, as is precisely exhibited in the papers herewith, marked F, G and H, and being lists of the killed and wounded. The killed outright numbered 369—the wounded 1,483, making an aggregate of 1,852.

The actual loss of the enemy will never be known; it may now only be conjectured. Their abandoned dead, as they were buried by our people where they fell, unfortunately, were not enumerated, but many parts of the field were thick with their corpses, as but few battle fields have ever been. The official reports of the enemy are expressly silent on this point, but still afford us data for an approximate estimate. Left almost in the dark, in respect to the losses of Hunter's and Heintzleman's Divisions—

first, longest and most hotly engaged—we are informed that Sherman's Brigade—Tyler's Division—suffered, in killed, wounded and missing, 609—that is, about 18 per cent. of the brigade. A regiment of Franklin's Brigade—Gorman's—lost 21 per cent. Griffin's (battery) loss was 30 per cent., and that of Keyes's Brigade, which was so handled by its commander, as to be exposed to only occasional volleys from our troops, was at least 10 per cent. To these facts add the repeated references in the reports of the more reticent commanders, to the "murderous" fire to which they were habitually exposed—the "pistol range" volleys, and galling musketry, of which they speak, as scourging their ranks, and we are warranted in placing the entire loss of the Federalists, at over forty-five hundred in killed, wounded and prisoners. To this may be legitimately added as a casualty of the battle, the thousands of fugitives from the field, who have never rejoined their regiments, and who are as much lost to the enemy's service as if slain or disabled by wounds. These may not be included under the head of "*missing,*" because, in every instance of such report, we took as many *prisoners* of those brigades or regiments as are reported "*missing.*"

A list appended exhibits some 1,460 of their wounded and others, who fell into our hands, and were sent to Richmond; some were sent to other points, so that the number of prisoners, including wounded, who did not die, may be set down as not less than 1,600. Besides these a considerable number, who could not be removed from the field, died at several farm houses and field hospitals within ten days following the battle.

To serve the future historian of this war, I will

note the fact, that among the captured Federalists, are officers and men of *forty-seven* regiments of volunteers, besides from some nine different regiments of regular troops, detachments of which were engaged. From their official reports, we learn of a regiment of volunteers engaged, six regiments of Miles's Division, and the five regiments of Runyon's Brigade, from which we have neither sound nor wounded prisoners. Making all allowances for mistakes, we are warranted in saying that the Federal Army consisted of at least fifty-five regiments of volunteers, eight companies of regular infantry, four of marines, nine of regular cavalry, and twelve batteries, forty-nine guns. These regiments, at one time, as will appear from a published list appended, marked "K," numbered in the aggregate 54,149, and average 964 each. From an order of the enemy's commander, however, dated July 13th, we learn that one hundred men from each regiment were directed to remain in charge of their respective camps—some allowance must further be made for the sick and details, which would reduce the average to eight hundred men—adding the regular cavalry, infantry and artillery present, an estimate of their force may be made.

A paper appended, marked "L," exhibits, in part, the ordnance and supplies captured—including some twenty-eight field pieces of the best character of arm, with over one hundred rounds of ammunittion for each gun, thirty-seven caissons, six forges, four battery wagons, sixty-four artillery horses, completely equipped, five hundred thousand rounds of small arms ammunition, four thousand five hundred setts of accoutrements, over five thousand muskets, some nine regimental and garrison flags, with a large number of pistols, knapsacks, swords, canteens, blankets; a large store of axes and entrenching tools, wagons, ambulances, horses, camp and garrison equipage, hospital stores, and some subsistence.

Added to these results, may rightly be noticed here, that by this battle an invading army, superbly equipped, within twenty miles of their base of operations, has been converted into one virtually besieged, and exclusively occupied for months in the construction of a stupendous series of fortifications for the protection of its own Capitol.

I beg to call attention to the reports of the several subordinate commanders for reference to the signal parts played by individuals of their respective commands. Contradictory statements, found in these reports, should not excite surprise, when we remember how difficult, if not impossible, it is to reconcile the narrations of by-standers or participants in even the most inconsiderable affair, much less the shifting, thrilling scenes of a battle field.

Accompanying are maps showing the positions of the armies on the morning of the 21st July, and of three several stages of the battle; also, of the line of Bull Run north of Blackburn's Ford. These maps, from actual surveys made by Captain D. B. Harris, assisted by Mr. John Grant, were drawn by the latter with a rare accuracy worthy of high commendation.

In conclusion, it is proper, and doubtless expected, that through this report my countrymen should be made acquainted with some of the sufficient causes that prevented the advance of our forces and prolonged, vigorous pursuit of the enemy to and beyond the Potomac. The War Department has been fully advised long since of all of those causes, some of which only are proper to be here communicated. An army, which had fought as ours on that day, against uncommon odds, under a July sun, most of the time without water and without food, except a hastily snatched, scanty meal at dawn, was not in condition for the toil of an eager, effective pursuit of an enemy immediately after the battle.

On the following day an unusually heavy and unintermitting fall of rain intervened to obstruct our advance, with reasonable prospect of fruitful results. Added to this, the want of a cavalry force, of sufficient numbers, made an efficient pursuit a military impossibility.

Respectfully, your obedient servant,
G. T. BEAUREGARD,
General Commanding.

To GENERAL S. COOPER, *Adjutant and Inspector General, Richmond, Va.*

(Official.) R. H. CHILTON,
Adjutant.

ERRATA.

Page 12—In regard to the cause which produced a junction of the command of General Johnston with that of General Beauregard, it is deemed necessary to add that the order of the former was discretionary, and amounted simply to permission to take this step, if, in his judgment, it should be necessary.

Page 29—Instead of General Smith having arrived from the cars, it should be stated that General Smith arrived from Manassas, in command of Elzey's Brigade. General Smith was wounded while placing his Brigade in position, when the command devolved upon Colonel Elzey.

Pages 30 and 60—Elzey's Brigade was composed of the 10th Virginia Regiment, Colonel S. B. Gibbons, the 1st Maryland, Colonel Elzey, and 3d Tennessee, Colonel Vaughan.

Pages 30 and 61—Early's Brigade; instead of "24th Virginia Regiment, Colonel Early," read the "13th Mississippi Regiment."

Page 73—Fifth line from the bottom, instead of "wounded," read "mounted."

Page 78—Ninth line from bottom of page, read "In silence long to rest," instead of "The spirit was released."

The 8th Georgia Regiment was not engaged with the enemy in the afternoon, or at the Henry House, as stated in this book.

www.ingramcontent.com/pod-product-compliance
Lightning Source LLC
Chambersburg PA
CBHW030255170426
43202CB00009B/747